Also by Erin N. O'Reilly published on Amazon

A Victorian Christmas Collection:
Holiday Recipes, Stories, and Quips from America's Gilded Age

Café Noir:
A Victorian Coffee Compendium

**Jokes from the 1800s
Volume I**

By E.N. O'Reilly

Copyright 2018

convivialsupper.com

Amazon Edition

Cover Art: Kansas Agitator

~~~~

Dedicated to Patrick.

A PERPETUAL MOTION PERAMBULATOR.

A GERMAN DEVICE FOR KEEPING A RESTLESS BABY ASLEEP.

—Fliegende Blätter.

Never Apologized.

There is a good story of a general whose death was printed in a paper by mistake, a circumstance which annoyed him very much. He called on the editor and demanded that a contradiction should be inserted in the next issue. "That, general," was the editor's reply, "is quite out of the question. We never apologize and we never withdraw a statement; but I tell you what we will do for you. We'll put you in the 'Births' next week."

Inequality.

"Mama, I saw a dog to-day that had only three legs."

"Were you awfully sorry for him?"

"No'm, he had one more leg than I had."

"I pity a man who is not beloved by children."

"Don't lavish too much sympathy on him; he can wear a linen suit all day and look respectable."

The Reason.

Boggs - How is it that your hair is quite white, while your beard is very dark?

Noggs - It's the most natural thing in the world.

Boggs - Indeed!

Noggs - It is thirty years older.

Signs of Proficiency.

"Have you made any progress in your music?" asked Maud.

"I'm doing splendidly," replied Mamie.

"Does your teacher say you are improving?"

"I know it without his telling me. The first family that moved into the house next door after I began to take lessons remained only three weeks. The next family stayed the month out. The next lived there six weeks, and the people occupying it now have been there two months, and don't scowl at the house as they go past it."

Dumb in All the Seven.

Wife - You do not tell me that Prof. A- has been struck dumb?

Husband - Yes, last night. He was master of seven languages.

Wife - Is it possible? And he was struck dumb in all seven?

Works Both Ways.

"So you've lost all your marbles, eh? Well, it serves you right. Boys always lose who play on Sundays."

"But how about the other feller who won all my marbles?"

Rather Crowded.

Aunt Prue - If you tell lies, Dicky, you will go to a bad place.

Dicky - Does everybody who tells lies?

Aunt Prue - Yes, Dicky, they all go there.

Dicky - Then I guess I ain't afraid much. It must be over-crowded now.

Interesting Orphans.

"Please, ma'am, won't you read the letter?"

The voice was that of a little boy by whose side stood a smaller child carrying a great basket upon his arm. The lady took the note and read: "Good person, please give these staring little ones - fatherless and motherless-a penny."

The reader regarded the beggars with tearful eyes as she inquired in a voice choked with emotion: "Who wrote this note for you, children?"

With a sniffle of expectancy the elder answered bravely, "Me muvver, ma'am!"

She - "You used to say you would think no more of me if I was worth lots of money."

He - "So I wouldn't; not a particle; not so much, in fact. I am afraid I should be thinking most of the time of the money."

What Did He Do Then?

He - If I should kiss you would you call your mother?

She (naively) - Why, no! She wouldn't care to be kissed.

"Say, wot's dis—Romeo et Juliette?"
"I dunno, unless Romeo was hungry."

There Are Others.
"To the stake with her!" thundered the tyrant.
"Mercy!" implored the unhappy captive. "Some other death! In heaven's name, some other death!" She entreated deaf ears and a heart of stone. "If he could only know," she moaned as she was dragged away, "how I hate to cook!"

Long Headed.
First Lady - I don't see how you can afford to let your lodgers owe you several weeks' rent.
Second Lady - Well, it's like this. When they're in debt it affects their appetites - they never like to ask for a second helping - so it comes cheapest in the end.

Not Useless.

Jones - The fire escapes in this house seem to be poor arrangements.

Smith - I don't know. They have enabled one man to escape.

Jones - Who was he?

Smith - A burglar.

Effective.

Maud - "What do you do when a man persists in asking for a dance and you don't care to dance with him?"

Marie - "Tell him my card is full."

Maud - "But supposing it isn't and he still persists?"

Marie - "Then I insist that it is and let him see that it isn't."

A Case of Cold Feet.

"My husband says your husband gets cold feet when he plays poker," said Mrs. Jack Potts.

"I don't wonder," replied Mrs. Luke Pleasant, "for whenever he does play poker he always comes upstairs in his socks."

Anticipatory.

"How can he be so rich, when he tried to borrow money off my brothers the day after we were engaged?"

"That was only a precautionary method. He wanted to prevent them from doing the same thing to him."

How It Happened.

"Great Scott!" exclaimed the young man from the city, who was inclined to be critical. "How terribly cross-eyed that half grown son of Farmer Whetrock is! He is certainly the worst case I ever saw. He looks as if one eye were gazing regretfully back at last Fourth of July, while the other was looking anxiously forward to next Christmas. What an unfortunate thing to be born so!"

"Oh, he wasn't born that way," replied Farmer Hornbeak. "One time, when the boy was about 9 years old, his father took him out in the woods and they saw a big gray squirrel up in a tree and a chipmunk friskin' around on the ground some distance to one side. The old man told the boy to stand perfectly still and keep his eyes fixed on both of them while he went back to the house for his gun. The boy obeyed orders so faithfully that by the time his father got back his eyes were twisted clear out of their base, and they've stayed that way ever since.

Unpleasant.

"I never met a more unpleasant fellow to play poker with than Jones."

"How's that? Does he get mad when he loses?"

"He never loses. That's what is so unpleasant."

Getting Off Cheaply.

Mrs. Commonstock, at summer hotel - They say the waiter at our table is a foreign nobleman.

Mr. Commonstock, excitedly - Good! I'll offer him one of our daughters and a share in my business and escape tipping him.

A Basis of Calculation

She arose, smiling, from the dentist's chair.

"How much do I owe you?" she asked.

"Three dollars and a half," was the reply.

"Are you sure that's right?" she inquired, suspiciously.

"Quite sure."

"Well, it seems a good deal. The time I was here before you only charged me two dollars, and you hurt me ever so much more than you did this time."

"Did you ever see anything lie deeper than the snow this winter?" the passenger from Canada was saying.

The passenger from main toyed reflectively with the corkscrew in his pocket. "Not unless we except the oldest inhabitant," he replied, after a thoughtful pause.

No Wonder the Teacher Was Puzzled.

Country schoolmasters have peculiar experiences sometimes. A pedagogue relates that one day he received from a small boy a slip of paper, which was supposed to contain an excuse for non-attendance of the small boy's big brother.

He examined the paper and saw thereon the word: "Cepatomtagotaturing."

Utterly unable to make out the puzzle, he appealed to the small boy, who explained that it meant that his brother had been "kept at home to go taturing -" that is, to dig potatoes.

Capacious.

Jenks - If America had the Mayflower, now, we could sweep England off the seas.

Hanks - What makes you think so?

Jenks - Because, according to the millions of people claiming their ancestors came over on the Mayflower, the ship must have been as big as the state of Illinois.

Absorbed.

The missionary thought he could
Free the cannibal chief from sin,
But his majesty was too smart for him,
And finally took him in.

An Up-to-Date Town.

"Many years ago," said the jubilee orator, "it was said of us that we were the inhabitants of a one-horse town. To-day we stand with the stigma removed. As we look forth on our streets and see the merry bicycle and the dignified gasoline carriage speeding to and fro, we say with conscious pride that we are a one-horse town no longer. The last horse has been banished, and we are a modern, up-to-date, no-horse town of the first class."

Strategic Mr. Chaffle.

Mrs. Chaffle - I don't know how I can get Johnnie to take his medicine. If I tell him what it is he won't take it, and if I don't tell him he won't take it.

Mr. Chaffle - I'll tell you what to do. Just put it on the table and forbid him to touch it, and then he will take it, sure.

It Cut Both Ways.

A young woman in a Maine town, who recently played cards for three hours one evening, died the next day, and a local clergyman took the incident as a text for a sermon in which he declared that her death was a judgment sent by God to indicate His condemnation of card playing. But the next week a man dropped dead while carrying food to a starving family, and his sudden death was declared to be an evidence of mercy and therefore took him home.

A City Innocent.

She was from the city, where the lawns are well watered and well kept, and was on a visit to the country, where the grass is mostly hay, and very dry and dusty even for hay.

"Papa," she said thoughtfully, "the people never try to water the grass out here, do they?"

"Of course not," he replied, "it would be too much of a task."

"They leave it all to God to look after, don't they?" she persisted.

He nodded his head, and for a few minutes she was lost in thought.

"Papa," she said finally, as if she had solved a great problem, "don't you think God ought to get an automatic sprinkler?"

New Border - "This rain is good for the farmer. Brings things up out of ground, you know."

Farmer - "Gosh, don't talk that way. I've just buried my third wife."

Why Postponed.

When the wedding notice appeared in the paper it was announced that the ceremony was necessarily postponed for several days owing to the non-arrival of the bride's trousers. The ignorant printer had misspelled the word trousseau.

A Dreadful Contingency

"Your money, and quick, too!" said the tall burglar.

"For goodness sake, don't make so much noise," hissed the unhappy householder as he sat up in bed.

"Why not?"

"You'll wake the baby."

The short burglar laughed brutally. He had heard the old gag when he was a child at his mother's knee.

"Wot if we do wake the baby?" said the tall burglar.

"If the baby cries," groaned the unhappy victim, "it will sour the temper of my wife's pet dog, and then there'll be Hades to pay."

With a glance of deep commiseration, the burglars softly stole away.

An Indispensable Personage.

"I guess we'd better fix up a flag of truce and show it to these Cubans," said the Spanish general.

"Is that absolutely necessary?"

"I'm afraid so. My stenographer wants a vacation."

Not to Be Expected.

Tourist—How long will it take me to reach the ferry, me good man?
Policeman—I ain't no mind reader, I'm a policeman.

Timely Wit.
"I don't want the wheel. It is too heavy."
"Say, I'll throw in a lamp. That'll make it lighter."

The Difference.
Small Boy - Pa, what is the difference between a pessimist and an optimist.

Pa - Well, let me see if I can illustrate. You know I am often discouraged, and things don't look to me as if they'd ever go right. Well, at such times I can be said to be a pessimist. But years ago, when I was a young man, everything looked bright and rosy and I was always hopeful. Then I was an optimist. Now, my son, can you understand the difference between a pessimist and an optimist?

Small Boy - Oh, yes; one is married and the other isn't.

Why They Fume.

They were laughing over at the courthouse about the way certain of the candidates for sheriff were raising merry tribulation. It is all because somebody told them that one of the clerks in the probate office was working for a rival candidate. This somebody claims to have overheard in a dialogue which runs something like this:

Candidate for marriage license, approaching window:
"I like to get married."
Affable Clerk - Certainly. Your name?
"Adolph Linkhammer."
"And age?"
"Thirty-two."
"The lady's name and age?"
"Mary Schwartzentroop; twenty-four."
"Yes. Are you a voter, Mr. Linkenhammer?"
"Oh, yes. Six years now."
"Where do you live?"
"Near Jackson Street."
"Pretty well acquainted there?"
"Yes, I know a good many."
"Ever take any interest in politics?"
"Oh, sometimes."
"Well, here are a few of Mr. McConnell's cards. He's a man we want for sheriff. Do what you can for him. I'll have the license ready for you in half a moment."
That's the story that makes the other candidates froth at the mouth.
But, then, other candidates do froth at the mouth so easily.

The Colonel's Idea of It.

The debate on social conditions and their remedies had been going on for some time, and Colonel Stillwell was getting very much in earnest. "What this country suffers from," he said, "is too much politics, sir. There are not enough men saying, 'What can I do for my country?' and too many saying, 'What can my country do for me' sir. We have too many office-holders, sir."

"I can't agree with you, colonel," said Senator Sorghum. It seems to me that the chief difficulty lies in the old discrepancy between supply and demand. As you say, there are too many office-holders."

"Exactly, sir."

"And not enough offices."

On the Wrong Side.

The Kentucky Colonel had just been rescued from a watery grave in the bottom of the Mississippi River.

"Where am I?" he asked feebly, as he opened his eyes.

"Safe on shore," replied one of the rescuers.

"On which side of the river?"

"The Iowa side."

For a moment the news seemed to overcome him, and he turned sorrowfully toward the river.

"Just my luck to land in a prohibition state," he said with a sigh, "Throw me in again."

The Way She Took It.

Mrs. Lovely (proudly) - Yes, Mr. Lovely and I have been married for twenty-five years. And we have yet to make up our first real quarrel.

Miss Pert - Isn't that rather a long time to sulk?

How Women Love Each Other.

Miss Bluestock—I tell you, man is but an earth-born worm.

Julie—You couldn't have been very lively as an early bird, my dear!

Her Last Request.

"One moment," said the fated Queen of Scots, as she paused at the foot of the scaffold, "I have a last request to make. When you come to bury me, and are about to restore my head to my body, be sure to remember one thing."

"And what is that?" quoth the impatient warder.

"Just try your best to put it on straight."
And the cortege swept on.

Justification.

"My dear," said Mrs. Dukane to her daughter, "I am inexpressibly shocked to hear you use such expressions."

"What expressions, mamma?"

"Didn't I hear you say to your brother, 'What's eating you?'"

"I guess you did."

"Well, don't you know that is very reprehensible slang?"

"But, mamma, isn't the word 'eat' a synonym for 'consume?'"

"Yes, I suppose it is."

"Then, mamma, dear, I don't think that your criticism is well founded for I have often heard you say you were consumed with curiosity."

The Distinction.

Tom - Then you disapprove of whiskers, Miss Gushingly?

Miss Gushingly - Oh, no, not at all.

Tom - But didn't you say as much?

Miss Gushingly - I only said, "It was a fashion that I invariably set my face against."

No Wonder.

Mrs. Talkalot - What makes you talk so much in your sleep, Joseph?

Joseph - Gosh! It's the only chance I ever get.

Mistress – "What a time you've been about that egg, Mary."
Mary – "Yes, ma'am; but the new kitchen clock has such large minutes!"

No Straddling.
Jaspar - "Lend me ten dollars, will you, old chap?"
Jumpuppe - "In gold or in silver?"
Jaspar - "Either. I don't care which."
Jumpuppe - "Get out! I won't lend a cent to a man who straddles on the financial question in these troubled times."

A Wise Method.
Mrs. Walker - "I don't see why the doctors all recommend bicycle riding. If it makes people healthier it is a loss to the doctors."
Mr. Walker - "I know; but they figure that one sound, healthy rider will disable at least five pedestrians per week.

An Iowa farmer bet a new hat that he could cross the railroad track with his team before the train came up. He was lost by ten feet. The distance was measured by his heirs.

Doomed to Be Disappointed.
"I shall be preserved," insisted the missionary, devoutly confident even in the hour of his peril. The cannibal shook his head. "I hate to disappoint him," mused the savage, "and even if the hot, muggy season of the year wasn't coming on, I wouldn't."

"Ratty taste," said the butcher, "can't understand it. Those sausages were not made of rats, sir, and you know it. May be the cats had caught and eaten a few, though."

Its Sad Remarks.

"Do you believe that money talks?"
"Certainly."
"What did it ever say to you?"
"It said: 'Ta, ta.' "—Up-to-Date.

Just the Thing.

Mrs. Doolittle (continuing story) - "And then their conduct became so very shameful, it is really unfit for decent ears to hear."

Mrs. Wigglesby (settling back with an air of delighted expectancy) - "Tell it!"

Never Meet.

Kidder - Although Corbett and Fitzsimmons differ a great deal in measurements (and opinion), they are built on parallel lines.

Kodder - How so?

Kidder - Why, they never meet.

Like the Rest.

Mrs. Brown - "Ah! If I was only a man!"

Mr. Brown - "You'd be just as foolish as men are - go and marry some idiotic woman. I'll bet a dollar."

A Matter of Age.

Mr. Youngly - "They say there is no fool like an old fool."

Miss Newvill - "But that saying originated before you were born."

Got Rid of the Chaperon.

"I thought I saw you riding alone with a gentleman last evening."

"You did."

"But does your mother let you go bicycling with a gentleman without a chaperon?"

"No indeed!"

"But you had none."

"Oh, we had when we started, but we punctured her tire to get rid of her."

He Was Cornered.

"Did you see me in the parade?" said Mr. Dolan to his wife.

"I did."

"Wasn't I a fine sight then?"

"You were indeed. I had to look twice to realize that the man that stepped along so lively and easy to the music was my own husband that wasn't able to walk around the corner to the grocery last night because of the rheumatism."

A Lucky Find.

Manager - You say you would like to get engagement as leading lady in my acting company. When were you divorced last?

Miss DeLyle - Three years ago.

Manager - I'm sorry I cannot take you. The public will have forgotten all about it by this time, and I really have no money to spare for extra advertising.

Miss DeLyle - But, you know Willie Bainbridge and Clarence Fernleigh are to fight a duel on my account next week.

Manager - Hurrah! Consider yourself engaged. Your name will be printed on the program in the largest letters they have, and your salary will be $450 a week. The success of the show is already assured.

A Fit Name.

Mother - Mr. Gayley made a very flattering remark about our girls last evening. Said they were all peaches - that we had a regular crop of peaches. Very flattering, was it not?

Father, sourly - I don't know about it being flattering at all. They are certainly a peach crop - a dead failure every year!

Wickwire - I see that another policeman has been suspended for sleeping on his watch.

Mudge - I have been eating and drinking on mine for a week.

A Slander.

"Is it true that your wife is an erudite woman?"

"Gracious, no! She knows too much to be that."

How He Lost His Eyesight.

"Poor man! How did you lose the sight of your eye?"

"Lookin' for work, mum!"—Pick-Me-Up.

A Ruse.

"What are those golf sticks for?" asked the manager of the small theatrical venture.

"That's a little idea of my own. We can use 'em when we're walking home and make believe that we're just out enjoying ourselves."

Know One of the Tricks.

I don't see what fun it can be for you to go on these fishing expeditions with your husband," said her best friend.

"That's because you don't know anything about fishing," she replied.

"Do you?"

"Oh, yes, indeed. I can sit in the stern of the boat, and give advice with the best of them, and when the fish gets away there's no one can beat me telling how it ought to have been landed."

"I shouldn't think that would be much fun."

"That's because you don't know how mad it makes my husband."

Vicissitudes of War.

"Bah," said the old soldier. "You never saw a battle, except in a picture."

"No," admitted the young man, "I never did. But I have been on the same street with a policeman who was shooting at a dog."

Two Wardrobes.

Loving Wife - "My summer wardrobe is completed, and I am now ready for Newport."

Husband - "Well, I'll see if I can arrange my affairs so I can go."

"Gracious! I can't take you along. You haven't a suit of clothes fit to be seen.

Prison Warden - "Four reporters from the New York papers to interview you, and the hangman is ready for you-"
Condemned Prisoner (hastily) - "Send in the hangman!"

He'd Done it Before.
"You look after the dimes," he said in his lordly manner at the conclusion of a few remarks on the cost of running a house, "and I'll look after the dollars."
"I've been looking after the dimes all my life," she protested indignantly, "that's all I've had to look after while you - you-"
"Maria," he cautioned, fearful that there was about to be an explosion.
"While you - you have been diligently looking after the dollars-"
His face relaxed in a grateful smile.
"To spend," she said in conclusion.
He realized then that she had made a study of him.

A Mystery.
"I'd like to ask one thing," said the cross border.
"What is it please?" asked the landlady.
"How did you get this steak cooked so hard without even getting it hot?"

Wear and Tear.
"The essential differences between the man and the woman," said the Cheerful Idiot, "is one of wear and tear."
"Eh?" said the new border.
"Yes. Man spends his money foolishly on a tear and woman on wear."

The reporter lay on his eiderdown couch, slowly breathing his life away. It was evident that the end was very near. Suddenly the luxuriously furnished room was filled with phosphorescent light, and a pale shade appeared, standing at the bedside, grim and inscrutable.

"I am the Messenger of Death!" he said.

"One moment, please!" gasped the reporter, reaching feebly for his notebook and pencil. "How do you like America?"

Couldn't Afford It.

Mrs. Cobwigger - I know it would do me the world of good to go away for the summer, but I couldn't think of letting you stay in the city.

Cobwigger - Are you afraid of sunstroke?

Mrs. Cobwigger - Not at all.

Cobwigger - Can it be possible that you are jealous?

Mrs. Cobwigger - Of you? The idea!

Cobwigger - Then what in the world can it be?

Mrs. Cobwigger - To tell you frankly, my dear, I don't think we can afford it. Just think what it means for a man to stay in town all summer who plays such a poor game of poker as you do.

The Law's Majesty.

Justice - You are charged with failing to provide for your motherless children, who are at this minute starving in your miserable home. How much money have you in your pockets?

Prisoner - Ten dollars.

Justice - You are fined ten dollars. Next case.

An Instantaneous Portrait.

"I am tired to death!" declared Mrs. Young, as she reached home from town the other evening.

"What's the matter?" asked her husband.

"'Been having baby's portrait taken. They have a way of taking them instantaneously now, you know."

"How long were you at it?"

"Three hours and a half."

A Still Hunt.

"I understand," said the squire, "that you went to the theater last night. Were the living pictures chaste?"

"Well," answered the neighbor reflectively, "they wan't chased, but they was throwed at considerable."

A Melancholy State.

"I've made up my mind to one thing," said the resolute looking young man. "I'm not going to the theater any this winter."

"What for?"

"For many reasons. In the first place, I can't afford it and if I could afford it I would probably find all the seats taken for the play I wanted to see. And if I got a seat it would be behind a girl with a big hat. And if I did get to see the play I might not like it, anyhow."

A Leading Question.

"Is your mamma home, my dear?"

"Yes sir."

"Well run and tell her that one of her old beaus would like

to see her."

"Please sir, which one are you?"

"Which one?"

"Yes sir. I heard papa telling mamma about all of you last night. He said one of you was hanged, and one was a forger, and one was a bigamist, and one a bunco steerer, and one ran a faro bank, and two were free lovers. Which one are you?"

She Merely Warned Him.

"Don't you dare talk to me about a woman's wanting the last word," said Mr. Meekton's wife.

"Henrietta," he postulated, "I haven't thought of talking about it."

"This is simply a warning for the future. I used to think that a woman was persistent in wanting the last word. But after hearing two men who stood under my window till 3 o'clock in the morning arguing finance it makes me ashamed of my sex to think how easily we get discouraged and quit.

An Amendment.

"Did you tell a friend of mine," the small man exclaimed indignantly, "that I could not tell the truth if I tried?"

"No sir," replied the large man. "I wouldn't think of saying anything like that."

"I am glad to hear it."

"I wouldn't think of saying you couldn't tell the truth if you tried, because-"

"Well?"

"So far as I am informed you never tried."

Handy.

Miss Citybred—Where is the milk-maid?

Farmer Waterbury—Well, I don't mind tellin' ye; a good bit of it is made right here, Miss Citybred.

Rotation of Crops.

Some American tourists were visiting an old monastery near Florence, and going through the grounds at last came to a spot which contained a large vegetable garden on one side, while on the other lay the cemetery of the fathers, a path dividing the burial place from the garden.

"How often do you change your garden over to the other side?" asked one of the party, with an attempt at facetiousness.

To his surprise the father gravely answered, "About once in twenty-five years."

He Got a Job.

Awkward Youth - Sa-ay, can't yer give me a job on this here paper? I don't 'spose I can learn to be an editor, but I'm told there is other sorts of work in newspaper offices.

Mr. Beatemall (great editor) - You might suit in some capacity, perhaps. Do you know anything about bookkeeping?

"Nope."

"Are you good at figures?"

"Ah, yes, I'm good at figgers."

"How much are 9 and 7?"

"Lemme see. Put down 9, and then put down 7 alongside of it, an that make 97."

"Well, sir, you would do for the counting room, but I see no reason why you should not rise to proud eminence in the circulation department."

Woman is a delusion and a snare; yet man, poor man, loves to be snared by a delusion.

A Great Game.

"Why, Jacky, open the door and let Katie in. Don't you see it's raining?" cried Jacky's mother.

"I can't, mamma," said Jacky, "we are playing Noah's Ark. I'm Noah and Katie is the sinners, and she must stay out in the wet."

A man can never tell what he will do in a pinch until a policeman pinches him.

Understood the Last.

She had bought some bric-a-brac and her husband was inspecting her. One of them was a small Asiatic idol, with an especially grotesque figure and an exceptionally hideous leer.

"Is that your ideal of beauty?" he said.

"There is no doubt at all that it is very artistic," she answered with a little indignation.

"Well, if that's what you consider attractive, I can at least understand how come you want me to wear the neckties you gave me on my birthday."

An Enviable Position.

"No, sir," said farmer Corntossel. "I'm not going to run for no office."

"Why not?" inquired the local statesman.

"There's too many in the business. They're runnin for president and vice president, and congress and more things than you can remember, all over the country. As soon as a man starts in to run for office he has to ask favors. I'm just goin' to keep out and let them go it, and the first thing me an two or three others will be the only ones left in this here country to enjoy the luxury of being coaxed."

Couldn't Afford It.

Bildad Jones - Father, can I go down to the cellar and get some apples to eat?

Farmer Jones - Yes, Bildad; but see you sort them all over first and don't pick out none but the bad ones.

Bildad - But suppose there ain't no bad ones, dad?

Farmer Jones - Then you'll have to wait till they get bad, Bildad. We can't afford to be eating good sound apples that's worth a dollar a bushel.

It Was the Cow's Fault

An Irish laborer who was somewhat new to his work was plowing one day and the furrows being somewhat uneven, the farmer told him to look at something at the other end of the field as a guide.

"That cow at the gate," he said "is right opposite us. Now, work straight for her."

"Right you are, sir," said Pat.

Coming back later on the farmer was quite horrified to find the plow had been traveling zigzag all over the field.

"How is this?" said he. "What have you been doing?"

"Sure sir," was Pat's reply, "I did what you told me. I worked straight for the cow, but the creature didn't keep still."

Why He Was Indignant.

A general, an old bachelor who usually dines in restaurants, had a habit of wiping his knife and fork on his napkin before eating. One day he was invited to a dinner party, and the hostess noticing this performance, told the waiter to bring him a fresh knife and fork. Again, he wiped them and again a fresh set was brought, whereupon the general turned and snarled at the waiter: "Idiot! Do you expect me to clean knives and forks for all the guests?"

Wanted Things Right.

The Cook - Please, ma'am, will you lend me your watch to boil the eggs?

Mistress - Why, Mary, you have clock in the kitchen, haven't you?

The Cook - Yes, ma'am; but the clock is slow, ma'am.

An ·Apt Answer.

Teacher—Johnny, you may tell me what is meant by capital punishment.
Johnny (speaking from experience) —That's what a feller gits fer commencin' his sentences with small letters.—Up to Date.

Tired of the Quiet.

Native - There's going to be an insurrection here soon.

Tourist - What's the trouble?

Native - Well, we haven't had any for about a month, and some friends of the president are getting up to save him from ennui.

His Punishment.

Artist (to a friend) - "I've sold my last picture to the rich pork-packer, Parvenu, for $500."

"I'm glad of it. The rascal deserves it."

Two Sides to the Case.

Mother (at a party) - Why did you allow young Saphead to kiss you in the conservatory?

Daughter - Why, ma!

Mother - Oh, you needn't "why, ma" me. One side of his nose is powdered and one side of yours isn't, and the people have noticed it.

On Hand When Not Wanted.

Mr. Cumso - "Cawker, does your wife ever lose her temper?"

Mr. Cawker - "Not permanently."

Not called on for Proof.

He - I claim to be a gentleman.

She - Aren't you glad you don't have to prove your claim?

Mrs. Bingo - Bobby, does the new little boy who has moved next door feel any more at home than he did?

Bobby - I guess he does. He has been home since we first met.

An Exchange of Compliments.

He - You may be engaged, but I can never conceive of your being in love.

She - And you may be in love, but I can never conceive of your being engaged.

Source of her Confidence.
Uncle George - I really can't understand you, Hattie. All the married women you know you say have mad bad matches, and yet you are quite ready to try matrimony yourself.
Hattie - Don't you know, Uncle George, that there's an excellent chance of getting a prize in a lottery where so many of the blanks have been drawn?

A Trying Occupation.
First Tramp - "Sometimes I wish I was a bartender."
Second Tramp - Oh, I donno. It must be kind of painful to be always passing over the liquor to other folks."

When a man finds his clothes are too loose, he should either change tailors or boarding houses.

Woman leads the world. She used smokeless powder for ages before man thought of trying to invent it.

Overdone.
Dukane - I don't know how you came to lose money in that scheme. You told me it was a rare investment.
Gaswell - The investment may have been a rare one, but I was well done before I got through with it.

Built Better Than He Knew.

Mrs. Jackson - I thought you told me you trimmed that hat yourself. I'm sure it is just as stylish as if it had been done by a high-priced milliner.

Mrs. Johnson (complacently) - Yes, I think it has a stylish look myself. You see, my husband sat down on it accidentally after I had got done and gave it exactly the right twist.

It does torment a railroad restaurant keeper frightfully to have a customer ask: "How much will you charge me a thousand for such sandwiches as these? I'm going to build a house, and I think they'd be more durable than brick."

"Talk about your ice machines," said a New Haven woman to her neighbor over the fence, "why, if Mrs. Robinson, round the corner, didn't treat me cool enough to freeze ice-cream this morning."

"Why, what did she say?"

"Say? She didn't say anything, and that's just what's the matter, and after I had taken pains to send her word that she was an impudent hussy." Aren't women curious critters?

A down-East militia Captain, on receiving a note from a lady, requested the "pleasure of his company," and understood it as a compliment to those under his command, and marched the whole of them to the lady's house!

His Preference.

Her father is a physician and an admirer of culture. But he grows weary now and then of hearing Mabel play scales and five finger exercises. After a half hour of work from her exercise book she turned and said, 'Father, I have taken up the study of theory."

"Have you?"

"Yes. This," she went on, striking a chord, "is a tonic."

"Mabel," he answered in a tone of patience sorely tried, "I'm ever so much obliged, but I don't think that is what I need. But if you had a sedative that you could try on me, I'd appreciate it more than tongue can tell."

Gained His Point.

In the days when her majesty went down to Windsor by road, she liked to be driven at a rapid pace - a little too fast to please her escort, especially the officers who rode their own horses. A gallant captain, afterward a renowned M.P., was one day in command and riding at the head of his troop. Just in front of him, with his back to the horses of the carriage, sat the Prince of Wales, then a small child. The captain, directly as the party started, lifted his hand and shook his fist in the little prince's face. The prince roared with fright, and his royal mother, quite ignorant of the cause, took him on her lap to pacify him. When the prince was quiet and resumed his seat, the captain again shook his fist, and this was repeated all the way down to Windsor. At the end of the journey the queen learned exactly what had occurred and issued her command that the officer should never command her escort again. This was just what the captain hoped would happen.

No Wonder He Was Begging.
"Can any of you tell me why Lazarus was a beggar?" asked the Sunday school teacher.
"Please, ma'am," replied a small boy whose father was a merchant, "because he didn't advertise."

Guided by Example.
"What's your name?" said the new school teacher, addressing the first boy on the bench.
"Jule Simpson," replied the lad.
"Not Jule - Julius," said the teacher. And addressing the next one, "What is your name?"
"Billious Simpson, I guess."

When a young lady hems a handkerchief for a wealthy bachelor, she probably sews that she may reap.

Encouraging.
She - Will you tell me a secret?
He - Why?
She - They say I can't keep one, and I want to try.

Practical.
Chawley Gotrocks - My dearest Margaret, I love you tenderly, devotedly. Your smiles would shed-
Margaret - Never mind the woodshed. How about a residence built for two?

Raison D'etre.

"I have at last discovered why daily papers are published."

"I didn't know there was any mystery about it. Isn't it to furnish the news to date?"

"No, indeed. The Monday, Tuesday, and Wednesday issues are to tell you what a grand paper they published last Sunday; and the Thursday, Friday and Saturday ones are to tell you what a magnificent one they're going to publish next Sunday."

Ought to Have Known It.

He - If I had known how sarcastic you were I never would have married you.

She - You had a chance to notice it. Didn't I say 'this is so sudden' when you proposed to me after two years of courtship?

Uncomfortably Cool.

Edith - Was Algy cool when he proposed?

Maude - I should say so! His teeth chattered.

Had Heard the Proverb.

Fond Parent - You had better go to bed now, Bobby, if you are going fishing in the morning, so that you can be an early bird tomorrow.

Bobby (decidedly) - Not me. The early bird has to catch the worms.

Rough on the Groom.

Mrs. Chatter—Nellie Gosling's wedding was a most brilliant one.

Mrs. Snappy—Humph! It doesn't seem to have brought her that sort of a husband!

Perhaps She Hadn't Thought of It.

"Well, said the sarcastic man as he walked out of the theater between acts, "I am ever so much obliged to the girl who sits in front of me. I don't know but I'll tell her so."

"You mean the one with the frightfully big hat?"

"Yes."

"I don't see what you are obliged to her for."

"For not raising her parasol."

Why He Made Music.

"Bobby is attending to his piano lessons very faithfully of late," said the youth's uncle.

"Yes," said his mother, "I don't have any trouble with him about that now."

"How do you manage?"

"Some of the neighbors complained about the noise his exercises made and I told him about it. Now he thinks it is fun to practice."

Tests.

"No, Mrs. Blimber, a woman is not fit to marry unless she knows how to cook."

"Then a man isn't fit to marry unless he knows how to saw wood."

Strange Circulation.

"Isn't it odd," asked Squildig, "that what I eat should go to my stomach, while what I drink goes to my head?"

"Yes," replied McSwilligen, "it is very strange that anything at all should go to your stomach while your head is so empty!"

A Father's Love Token.

"The development of the back of the head, my friends, indicate parental affection," explained the phrenologist. "Now you will observe," he went on, feeling the head of the boy on the platform, "that this bump is abnormal in size, thus indicating that this lad loves and reveres his parents to an unusual degree. Is it not so, my lad?"

"Naw."

"What? You do not love your parents?"

"I think well enough of mother," the boy replied, "but I ain't very fond of father. That bump you're feeling he gave me last night with a baseball bat."

A blind musician in East Liverpool, Ohio, has married a Chicago belle. It is perhaps unnecessary to mention his blindness.

Well Roasted.

Blathers - Say, did you find anything well roasted at the barbecue?

Slathers - Well, nothing except for management.

It is a singular fact that an 8-year-old boy is always more than two years younger when his mother takes him with her on a street car.

Unprofitable Virtue.

"Naw," said Tommy, "I ain't working the good little boy racket this Christmas; not much. I tried it last Christmas."

"Did they get onto you?" asked Jimmy.

"Naw, they didn't get onto me, but they thought I was in earnest, and went and bought me a dinky lot of Sunday school books and a set of chessmen."

It Makes a Difference.

"Miss Blank doesn't seem to be so enthusiastic about the new woman business as she was."

"No. She hasn't found it quite so much fun as it seemed at the beginning. While she was just striving for recognition, it was great sport, but now - "

"Yes?"

"Well, since she has received recognition to the extent that she has had to stand up in the street cars, hustle for her own theater tickets, and buy her own flowers, I have noticed that she has not been so emphatic in her demand for absolute equality."

No Reward Offered.

"What do they mean by 'Virtue has its own reward?'"

"I suppose they mean it's no use advertising when it's lost."

Celestial Fashion.

"When I married you," he said, "I thought you were an angel."

"I inferred as much," she said. "From the very first," she went on, "you seemed to think I could get along without clothes.

His Predicament.

"Never talk shop at home. A man should never mix his home and his business affairs."

"But I can't help it."

"Why not?"

"I edit the housekeepers' column of a family paper."

Friction.

She - I suppose it's hereditary that makes pugs' noses so short.

He - Yes, being kissed there for so many generations.

Good Advice.

"Mr. X has threatened to kick me next time he meets me in society. If I see him walk in what should I do?"

"Sit down."

Remarkable Confidence.

She: "It is remarkable what confidence that Mrs. Storms has in her husband! She believes everything he says."
He: "Well, why should she?"
She: "Why, man! He's a clerk in the weather bureau."

His Cure for It.

"When you want to get something from your husband by crying for it, what does he do?"
"He generally buys me a dozen handkerchiefs."

Too True.

Edith - "Matches are made in heaven, Grace."
Grace - "But on earth we make light of them."

Why is it when a woman wants to be considered literary, she cuts her hair, while a man for the same reason lets his grow?

He Gained Weight.

"Talk about your Western air to build up a man," said Charlie, "why I know a fellow who went out there about two years ago and gained over ten pounds a week."
"Holy smoke! Is it possible?"
"Yep. He sprang an old joke on the cowboys and they filled him full of lead."

Did the Right Thing.

Cleverton - If I had known that you were going to call on me, old man, I would have laid in some cigars.

Dashaway - I thought it was just as well to take you by surprise.

What Did He Mean?

"Do you know," remarked the author, "that I look upon my work as extremely valuable?"

"Why so?"

"A burglar was in the house the other night and stole $1.47, about $20 worth of jewelry and the manuscript of my latest story. I fear I shall never get the last back, but I will have justice on that burglar if we ever catch him."

"My dear sir, no jury would ever convict him."

"Why not?"

"He would be regarded as a public benefactor."

And the author has been trying to figure out the other's meaning ever since.

A Poor Trade.

Maud Muller on a summer's day, Raked the meadow, sweet with hay. A summer boarder whose words were fair, she married, and went away from there. And she wished she'd remained when she saw her mistake, wed to that other kind of rake.

Frequently when a woman gets a dream of a bonnet, her husband is tormented with a nightmare of a bill.

Metaphysical.

"Pat," said Tommy to the gardener, "what is nothing?"
"There ain't such a thing as nothing," replied Pat, "because when ye find nothin' and come to look at it there ain't nothin' there."

Too Inquisitive.

Pa - Well, Johnny, how do you like school?
Johnny - Oh, the school's all O.K., but the teacher doesn't know nothing'.
"Doesn't know anything? Why do you say that?"
"'Cause she's always asking us questions."

Unreasonable.

Tourist - In the East there is a law against carrying concealed weapons.
Westerner - So they expect one to go around all the time with a gun in hand?

A few days ago, a tramp stopped at a house in Garnett and told the lady of the house that if she would give him his breakfast he would saw some wood. She invited him in and gave him his breakfast and went to another room for a short time. When she returned, the tramp was gone and the following note was on the table: Just tell them that you saw me, but you didn't see me saw.

An Exception.
"You can't always tell a man by the company he keeps."
"Why not?"
"Why, there's Burger, for instance, just as nice a fellow as ever lived."
"But what about him?"
"Why, he was nominated for the Legislature."

Old Heads in Council.
Young Father - I've just made a big deposit in a savings bank, in trust for my baby boy. When he is 21, I will hand him the bank book, tell him the amount of the original deposit and let him see how things count up at compound interest.
Old Gentleman - Won't pay. I tried that. My boy drew the money and got married with it and now I've got to support him and his wife and eight children.

Poor Pasturage.
"Just thirty-three years ago to-day," said the old soldier, "the top of my head was grazed by a bullet."
"There isn't much grazing there now, is there, grandpa?" was the comment of the youngest grandchild, and as the old gentleman rubbed his bare poll he had to admit the correctness of the assertion.

Was a Victim Himself.
Winks - Do you believe in hypnotism?
Blinks - Of course I do. Don't you see this necktie that the clerk induced my wife to buy the other day?

The Old Lady Was Wise.

Sweet Girl – "Mother, Mr. Nicefellow is coming to take me out riding this afternoon. I may go, mayn't I?"

Mother – "If he drives up with a span of spirited horses you can go; but if he comes with that broken-down old nag he had last time, you shan't."

"Why, mother, I didn't suppose you would have such foolish pride."

"My dear, a young man who comes with a span of spirited horses expects to drive with both hands."

A Compromise.

Shopkeeper - What can I show you, sir?

Absent-minded Professor - I want - let me see, what do I want? Dear me! I can't for the life of me remember what it is. ...Well, well, it doesn't matter; give me the nearest thing you have to it.

Unanswerable.

Mamma - Oh, Ethel, don't ask mamma so many unnecessary questions!

Ethel - But, mamma, what can I ask you if I don't ask questions?

Her Invariable Rule.

"I don't believe in long engagements," said Miss Smatter.

"Neither do I," replied Miss Kittish. "Short engagements with plenty of them is my motto."

And He Fled.

Big Dog—Hello! there comes the dog catcher.

Little Dog—Well, I'll be dog-gone.—

An Inquiring Mind.

Bangs - From the West, eh?

"Yes, sir; from Chicago."

"Ah, indeed! I spent several months in Chicago. Been there long?"

"Yes, sir. I am a member of the city council."

"You don't say so? What street is your saloon on?"

His Strange Resemblance.

A certain farmer, who is by no means noted for his resemblance to Apollo, has a son of 7 who possesses more wit than pedigree. One day a stranger came to the farm, and, seeing the lad, asked:

"Sonny, where's your father?"

"In the pig pen," was the reply."

"In the pig pen? Thanks!"

And, as the man moved in the direction indicated, the boy shouted:

"I say! You'll know him, 'cause he's got a hat on!'"

Sometimes.

Bacon - I was reading to-day of a violin maker who made over 7,000 fiddles in his life.

Egbert - It's a fact, then, that the evil a man does lives after him.

Good for the Health.

Jinks (who has taken to horseback riding and bounces about ten inches at every step) - Ah, howdy do, Blinks? I think horseback riding is good for the health, don't you?

Blinks - Yes, indeed. All who see you will be benefited. Laugh and grow fat, you know.

What He Did Know.

Inquiring Spectator - Which horse was it that won?

Speculative Spectator (gloomily) - I don't know the name of the horse that won, but I know the name of most of the horses that didn't win.

Gen. Grant's Reply.

To a young lady who declared that Kentucky produced the handsomest women, the fastest horses, and the best whisky on earth, General Grant once made the reply: "I unequivocally indorse the first part of your statement. As to the horses, I admit that also, for I own some of them myself, and I am considered a good judge of horseflesh. But as to the whisky, you will pardon me if I doubt your position. Whisky, in order to be good, must be old, and your Kentucky men drink it up so fast that it doesn't have time to get old.

Jumping at Conclusions.

The Minister - Brother Brown, I understand that you attended the Adelphi theater this week. I cannot tell you how deeply pained I am to hear this.

Brother Brown - But I thought you didn't object to the theater on principle - that you merely condemned the objectionable shows.

The Minister - That, alas, is just it! This must have been a particularly disreputable performance. Why, I am told that they had the "Standing Room Only" sign out every night!

Weyler's Warfare.

"Give me my writing material," said Weyler to his secretary.

"Red or black ink, sir?"

"Red, you fool! I'm going to fight a battle!"

Favorable Sign.

Miss Robson - I don't think Fred will be long in coming to the point now.

Mrs. Robson - Why not?

Miss Robson - Because he's just beginning to worry about your bad temper.

His Philosophy.

The Nabob—"Selfish? Uncharitable! Why, my immense fortune keeps me so busy that I haven't time to think of other people."—Le Rire.

Natural Philosophy.

"What would you call the sound produced when two bodies come together?" asked the teacher, who was trying to explain what a noise is to her pupils.

"Oh, a kiss, ma'am," replied the little girl, who evidently had older sisters.

Thought Not.

Wyld - Is Higbee married?

Mack - No.

Wyld - I thought not.

Mack - Why?

Wyld - He is always singing "Home Sweet Home."

Never meddle with another man's business - unless you see your way clear to making something out of it.

Can it be that a sailor always speaks of a ship as "she" because it is so hard to manage her?

Might Be Mistaken.
She - If I were to die you would never get another wife like me.
He - What makes you think I'd ever want another like you?

Some preachers would like to preach Christ, but the great trouble is they have never managed to get acquainted with their subject.

A Cure.
Jones - Sillibub has a medicine which he declares is a sure cure for heart disease.
Smith - Did it cure him?
Jones - Yes; it gave him such a frightful attack of indigestion that he forgot all about his heart.

A Narrow Escape.
The company had assembled in the church, but the bridegroom was nowhere to be found. Finally, a messenger announced that the young man had been run over and killed while on his way to the church.

"And just think," she said, a month afterwards to a friend, "what a narrow escape I had from becoming a widow."

Will Investigate.
Doctor - Do you sleep with your mouth open?
Patient - Sure I don't know, doctor. I've never seen myself when I've been asleep, but I'll have a look tonight!

Tit for Tat.
He (angrily) - Was there any fool sweet on you before I married you?
She - Yes, one.
He - I'm sorry you rejected him.
She - But I didn't reject him; I married him.

Skinerman - But why did Jorkins commit suicide? He only had embezzled $800 and was safe in Mexico.
Talkerton - It was the disgrace of the thing. Jorkins had many an opportunity to get away with $100,000.

Essentials for a Husband.
"There are six necessities, you know, for a happy marriage."
"What are they?"
"First, a good husband."
"And the others?"
"The other five are money."

Freddy - What is a fad, papa?

Papa - A fad, my son, is a fashion gone stark mad.

Useful Lessons.

Jay Hayceded - Gosh, Maria, I guess I'll send that lazy college boy of ours to this here new school.

Maria - What school?

Jay - Here's a notice in the paper about a man that gives lessons in fencin'.

Not So Much Difference.

"And in conclusion," said the political orator, as he finished his speech, "in the language of a certain well known patriot, we want to know whether you are 'wid us or again' us.'"

"Did you ever hear such impertinence?" said Miss Leftover in high indignation.

She was hard of hearing.

"What is the matter?" asked Miss Dainty.

"The man has the impudence to ask whether we are widows or beginners."

What Two Dollars Will Do.

Tramp - Please, sir, a couple of dollars would give me a nice, comfortable home for the winter.

Benevolent Party - It would? Well, no man shall suffer all winter long for the sake of two dollars. Here's the money.

"Thankee, sir."

"But stop. How is that amount to give you a home?"

"It'll get me howlin' drunk, sir, and then the police and the judge will retire me to winter quarters, sir."

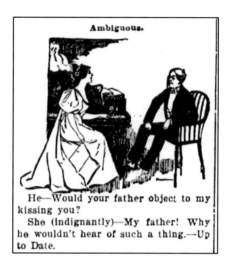

Ambiguous.

He—Would your father object to my kissing you?

She (indignantly)—My father! Why he wouldn't hear of such a thing.—Up to Date.

A Winter Paradox.

Jack - Miss Stateleigh was skating last night.

Tom - Was she as cold as ever?

Jack - Well, not quite so cold as she was last summer.

Query of the Times.

The lover was enthusiastic.

"She has poetry in her eyes," he exclaimed.

"Yes?" returned the cynic tantalizingly.

"She has roses in her cheeks," persisted the lover.

"Yes?" returned the cynic again.

"She has music in her voice," asserted the lover defiantly.

"And what in the bank?" queried the cynic.

Connubial Mysteries.

"A man who is just married tells his wife everything."

"Yes."

"And after he gets acquainted with her he doesn't tell her anything."

Contentment.

"What are you reading about?" asked Mrs. Corntossel.

"Diamond beds in Africa," replied her husband.

"Deary me. It doesn't beat all how much luxury these people manage to crowd into a lifetime. But I don't envy them. Not a bit. I don't ask for no greater comfort in the way of sleeping than plain, old-fashioned feather beds in winter and husks in summer."

Physical Phenomena.

"Why didn't Johnny shovel off the walk? Demanded Mr. Simpkins, as he brushed the snow off his trousers and dug some lumps of it out of his shoe tops.

"The poor boy's back was so lame, I hadn't the heart to make him do it," explained Mrs. Simpkins, apologetically.

"Huh! Where is he now?" he demanded.

"I don't know, I'm sure. I guess - yes, that's him over there with the Williams boy, rolling those big balls to make a fort."

Not Much Left to Lose.

The sea was pretty rough, the ship was pretty rocky, and the sick passenger was leaning against the rail. "Be careful," cautioned the officer, "or you will lose your balance." The passenger went through two or three spasms. "Well," he replied, "if this thing keeps up there won't be much balance to lose."

Example and Precept.

Friend - "How are you getting along these days, old fellow?"

Author - "Very poorly. Living between the hand and the mouth."

F. - "I thought so from your appearance. Why don't you give up writing and go into some kind of business in which you can earn a comfortable living?"

A.- "I've often thought of doing so, but the hope of one day making a strike, as you business men call it, keeps me at the pen. However, my new book may bring me in something handsome."

F. - "You are writing a book, then?"

A. - "Yes."

F. - "What's the title?"

A. - "How to Become Rich."

A Vicarious Transgression.

Father - "Johnny, I don't want to see this man. Run down and tell him I'm not at home."

Johnny - "But, father - I thought you never told lies."

Father (solemnly) - "I don't, my boy. It's you that's going to tell the lie."

Not Half.

Artist - I flatter myself; this last picture of mine is an excellent one.

Another Artist - My dear fellow, you don't flatter yourself half as much as you flatter the picture.

Plain Directions.

Mick (writing)—"Dear Bridget: If I ain't back before I comes, I shall arrive as soon as I get there, so mind and don't miss me when we meet."

Putting it Plausibly.

She - Did you have any trouble in getting papa to listen to you?

He - Not a bit. I began by telling him I knew of a plan whereby he could save money.

Worse Than That.

"Mrs. Rooney," said the Rev. Father McMurphy, "why do I never see Patrick at church now?"

Mrs. Rooney shook her head sadly.

"Is it anarchism?"

"Worse than that, your Reverence."

"Is it atheism?"

"Worse, your reverence."

"What is it, then?"

"Rheumatism."

The Safe Way.

Scadds - I've made half a million out of the stock market.

Spatts - Tell me how.

Scadds - By keeping out.

It's His Business.

"Isn't it a disgraceful surprise to see persons whom you would take to be reputable citizens procure themselves on the witness stand to save the worthless life of a murder?"

"Perhaps, but think of the depravity of a lawyer who hires them to do this."

"Yes, but there's no surprise in that."

Obliging.

"Madam," said Meandering Mike, "have you got any cold coffee?"

"No," replied young Mrs. Torkins in a tone of sympathy, "but you wait a few minutes and I will put some on the refrigerator to cool for you."

Only Partly True.

Mrs. Brown, indignantly - Is it true that he said that I was "fair, fat and forty?"

Mrs. Jones - I am not sure that he said "fair."

An Important Difference.

Prospective Litigant - You give legal advice here, don't you?

Lawyer, absentmindedly - No; we sell it.

Tommy's Sentence.

"Now, Tommy," said the teacher, "write me a sentence in which the words pine and butternut are used."

And Thomas wrote: "The fellow felt almighty tough when him his best girl cut; first he thought he'd pine away, and then he thought he'd butternut."

The Beauty of Them.

She (at the fire) - Horrors! Look there! A man is trapped on the top floor of the burning building. He - What in thunder is he excited about! The fire won't reach him for several years yet. That's the beauty of these tall office buildings.

Made Him Mad, Too.

Scribbler - "I have quite a passion for poetry, you know."
Editor - "I have the passion, too, when I read some of yours."

Did Not Amount to Much.

Visitor - I'm grieved to learn of your mistress's illness. Nothing serious - no great cause for alarm, I trust?
The New French Maid - No, monsieur; nozzing beeg, nozzing grande. Something what you call leetle, petite. What zey call ze leetle - small-small - smallpox.

"My cousin Josephine suffers from weak heart action."
"Weak heart action? Didn't I understand you to say she had been married four times?"

At the Ball.

Doll—Have you seen Maude? She's disguised herself completely.
Dick—How did she do it?
Dolly—Oh, she left off her makeup.

War Getting Out of Date.

"It won't be long," said the thoughtful man, "before all possibility of war among civilized nations will vanish forever."

"I quite agree with you," returned the member of the peace commission, grasping his hand and shaking it warmly. "We have unquestionably done noble work."

"You!" exclaimed the thoughtful man. "What have you done?"

"Not very much personally, perhaps, but as a member of the peace commission - "

"Peace commission nothing," interrupted the thoughtful

man. "The thing that is going to end all war is the fact that they have reached that point in the construction of mammoth cannons where a new national debt is created every time one is discharged."

Men Still Lead.
She (petulantly) - Women occupying front seats in a theater who take off their hats show as much consideration of others as men do.
He - No, they don't. Many men in the front row don't even wear any hair on their heads.

Ready for Orders.
"In summer time," said the loud voiced man in the street car, "you should drink the coldest water and keep all your eatables cold."
"I suppose you are a doctor?" said the lady next to him.
"No, madam; an ice dealer."

One Room as Good as Another.
A company of tourists are taken over the castle at Blois.
Guide - "The room which we are now entering, ladies and gentlemen, is the very one in which the Duke of Guise was murdered."
A Tourist - "Here, what's that? I came here three years ago, and was shown a room in the wing opposite."
Guide (very calmly) - "This room was undergoing repairs at the time."

As Usual.

"And did the groom kiss the bride?"

"Oh, yes."

"Before everybody?"

"No, after everybody except the sexton and the organist."

Future Hopes.

Bessie - I did not see you all last summer. I suppose you were very much engaged?

Louise - No, only to about five fellows, but I hope to do better this season.

He Knew the Law.

Johnnie's Teacher - And now, Johnnie, tell me what the last commandment is.

Johnnie (a street car tourist) - "Please don't spit on the floor."

Spring House Cleaning.

"Are you going to have your house painted this spring, Mudger?"

"No; but I'll have to paint the back fence, or the pump, or something. Mrs. Mudger never thinks she has cleaned house unless she can smell new paint."

Leading Symptom of "Sweating."

The leading symptom of "sweating" is low wages, usually wages so small as to make the incessant labor of man.

Too Slow.

"Why do you think that Bunker doesn't know his business?"

"Because it's nearly three years now since he's had a grand annual clearance sale."

A Distinction.

She - Then a 'tariff tinker' is a man who wants to make changes in the tariff?

He - Yes-that is, changes which we oppose. If he wanted to make the changes which we advocate, he'd be a statesman.

An Attractive Offer.

"Harold," said Harold's rich uncle, "if you will only stop smoking cigarettes, I'll begin smoking them myself and shorten my life by at least ten years."

Changed the Subject.

Adolphus Sofleigh - "Ah, my dear Miss Edith, you do not dream how many sordid men would seek to marry such an innocent, trusting girl as you are, just for her money. But I hope the man who wins you will love you for your own sweet sake alone."

Miss Edith - "Indeed, he will have to. It's my cousin - whose name is the same as mine - who is rich. I haven't a dollar of my own."

Adolphus (after an awkward pause) - "What strange weather we are having lately."

A Too Sensitive Ear.
Jones - "Great guns! You're getting deaf, old man."
Smith - "I'm not. I could never hear better in my life."
Jones, producing a watch - "Can you hear that watch tick?"
Smith, triumphantly - "Distinctly."
Jones - "That's queer. The watch isn't running."

Opportunity of a Lifetime.
He had called for the answer she had promised to give him,
but she looked at him doubtingly.
"It is a most momentous question," she said shyly. "I have
been studying my heart since yesterday, and I find that I am
very fond of you; but - but-"
"Yes," he put in anxiously, as she paused.
"This, you know, is a business world, and those who have
been guided solely by their hearts have not always done
well," she explained. "I am not mercenary, but there are
many things to be considered. If I agree to become your
wife what kind of future can you offer me
"Oh, as to that," he replied cheerfully, "you surely know
that I am a lawyer, and can save you attorney fees if you
ever want to get a divorce."

Two Views.
"Plunks is all torn up about that burglary."
"Yes, and Mrs. Plunks is tickled to death because now
everybody knows that she had seven dozen silver spoons to
be stolen."

Buncoed.

The elephant trumpeted loudly.

"What's the trouble?" asked the chimpanzee.

"Somebody's worked the shell game on me," replied the pachyderm, as he threw away the bag of empty peanut shells which had just been handed him.

A Trifle Enlarged.

"Sawyer seems to think a good deal of himself."

"I should say so. He has had a Moorish arch cut over his office doorway so he can get his head in and out."

"I understand, Grumpy, that your wife was shut up in a folding bed."

"Shut up? Nothing on earth can shut that woman up. She yelled till the policeman on the next beat heard her."

A Warning.

Author - What did you think of my play?

Critic - Great! Old man. Funniest thing I ever saw.

Author - Funny? Why, good heavens, man, it's a tragedy.

Mick (writing) – "Dear Bridget: If I ain't back before I comes, I shall arrive as soon as I get there, so mind and don't miss me when we meet."

Escaped.
"Have you ever had hay fever?"
"No; I always sleep on a straw bed."

Unanswerable.
"My grandfather," said Ribbs, "died at the age of 94."
"My grandmother was 103 when she died," remarked
Dibbs.
"And in my family," put in Tompkins, not to be outdone in
boasting, "are several aren't dead yet."

Almost the Same.
Nonie - Is your husband as shy now as he was before you
married him?
Laura - Almost, for then he used to hold his breath with
fear, and he does it just the same now when he comes home
late from the club.

An Ungallant Philosopher.
"I suppose," said the man whose hobby is economy, "that
as people advance in years they increase in wisdom. But I
have my doubts."
"I'm sure that I have more practical views of life than I had
some years ago," replied his wife.
"I won't dispute it. But the unalterable fact remains that a
7-year-old girl will be perfectly happy on Easter with a few
hard-boiled eggs, which are inexpensive and good to eat,
while a 27-year-old girl cannot exist without a high-priced
hat, whose only function is to make some woman jealous in
church, or some man miserable in the theater."

Ought to Do Well.

"If trouble is brewing," he said thoughtfully, "it certainly ought to do well."

He paused and they looked at him inquiringly.

"So far as my observation goes," he explained, "the brewers are generally prosperous."

A Foolhardy Experiment.

"Did you hear about Hawkins getting smothered in his morning mail?"

"Gracious, no! How did it happen?"

"He advertised for the names of persons contemplating the purchase of a bicycle."

The Truth of the Matter.

Miss Jolliet - It isn't true, Mr. Cynicus, that a woman cannot keep a secret.

Cynicus - I agree with you; but the trouble is that she cannot disguise the fact that she is keeping one.

A lantern-jawed young man stopped at Alva post office the other day and yelled out: "Any mail for the Wattses?"

The polite postmistress replied: "No there is not."

"Nothing? Anything for Charlie Watt?"

"No, sir."

"Anything for Maggie Watt?"

"No; nothing."

"Anything for Fool Watt?"

"No; nor for Dick Watt, nor Jim Watt, nor Sweet Watt, nor any other Watt, dead, living, unborn, native, foreign, civilized or uncivilized, educated or uneducated, male or female, white or black, franchised or disfranchised, naturalized or unnaturalized. No; there is positively nothing for any, now and forever, one and inseparable."

The man looked at the postmistress and said: "Please look and see if there is anything for Thomas Edgar Watt?"

Half-Price.

Dusty Dick - Say, boss, ain't you got a half a dollar for a blind chap?

Old Gentleman - Why, you're only blind in one eye!

Dusty Dick - All right, boss, make it 25 cents, then.

Quite Probable.

She - How do you account for the enormous increase in the English sparrows in America?

He - They're too ugly to go on women's hats.

Night on the Avenue.

Young Burglar (in the parlor) – Hark! I just heard the lady upstairs tell her husband that there were burglars in the house.

Old Burglar - That's all right. If they know we are burglars, they'll keep quiet, for fear of being killed. I was afraid they'd mistake us for poor relations and yell for the police.

They Pay More.
Little Willie - Say, pa?
Pa - Well, what is it?
Little Willie - Why do they always weigh babies as soon as they are born? Do people pay for them by the pound, the same as for raw meat?

His Everyday Wife.
"Does your wife take any interest in current politics?" asked the earnest woman.
"Naw," replied Mr. Sodfarm, "she don't. But if its currant jelly or currant pie, why I allow she could tell you more things about them than you ever dreamt of."

At Waterloo.
It was just previous to the battle of Waterloo. The Duke of Wellington was eating. Before he finished his repast, he remarked: "I enjoyed that meat, especially the Bonaparte, and now of Corsican go some pastry. Bring me a Napoleon."
After the battle was over, he said of the opposing general: "Waterlooser he was."

The Author Appeared.
Crissip - I hear that Scrawl had to make a speech at the first presentation of his play last night. What did he say?
Dale - He said if the audience would not tear up the seats they could have their money back.

They'd Leave.

First Nighter—"What! Every seat taken?"

Ticket Seller—"Every one; but there will be plenty after the first act—I saw a rehearsal."

Only a Bald Head.

Telescope Proprietor - Step up, ladies and gents, and view the planet Mars. One penny, mum.

Old Lady - Oh, law! Ain't it round and smooth!

Telescope Proprietor - Will the bald headed gent please step away from in front of the instrument?

They Do Things Differently.

Englishman - I see that a man was robbed in Central Park in broad daylight. Such things don't happen in London.

New Yorker - I suppose not. I've heard that broad daylight is a very rare occurrence there.

A Question of Value.

"It seems to me," said Mr. Severed to Attorney Cuttem, "that $100 is a very exorbitant fee for obtaining a divorce."

"It is our usual charge, sir, when the suit is not opposed. It is more if there is opposition to overcome."

"But I paid the minister only $10 for marrying me. Your charge seems out of proportion to his."

"It does not seem so to me, sir. Just compare the relative benefits arising from the respective services."

A Continuous Performance.

Mandy - Come on, Silas; it costs too much to eat in that place.

Silas - Yes, 50 cents is a lot to pay for dinner, but look how long we can eat - from 1:30 to 8 o'clock. Let's go in.

Pawson's Trouble.

"Pawson is in a dreadful dilemma, poor fellow!"

"What is the trouble?"

"He snores so loudly that he can't sleep."

A St. Louis man claims to have invented an electric eardrum which will make the deaf hear. The deaf have heard of these things before.

"Why are you looking so serious, Bobby?" asked the fond father.

"Thinking about the preacher. He went and told us we

should not covet other people's things, and then tried to get all the pennies we had."

The Colonel - So poor old Mike has committed suicide, has he? Well, I should have thought that would have been the last thing he'd have done.

Tenant - Which it were, sir.

He Heard It.

Uncle Josh (on a visit) - Where are the children?

Mrs. Witherspoon - Playing tennis in the garden.

Uncle Josh - How do you play tennis.

Mrs. Witherspoon - With a racket, of course.

Uncle Josh - That's so. I can hear it now.

Started the Thing Going.

An awkward affair is said to have occurred on Tuesday last outside the office of a Chicago paper. The editor of that paper had just left the office when a man rushed up, and, without so much as a "By your leave," knocked off the editor's hat, and trampled it under foot. The editor asked why. "You published an article the other day," came the answer, "in favor of the abolition of silk hats, didn't you?" "Yes," said the editor.

"Well, I've abolished yours," explained the fellow, "that's all."

Only One on His Side.

A well-known judge, noted for his tendency to explain things to juries, expressed in a recent case his own ideas with such force that he was surprised the jurors thought of leaving the box. They did leave, however, and were out for hours. Inquiring the trouble, the judge was told one of the twelve was standing out against the eleven. He summoned the jury and rebuked the recalcitrant sharply. "Your honor," said the juror, "may I say a word?"

"Yes, sir," said the indignant judge: "what have you to say?"

"Well, what I wanted to say is, I'm the only fellow that's on your side."

Too Bad, Indeed.

"Queen Victoria wears the same style of bonnet she did thirty years ago."

"Say, it's too bad a woman like that is a widow."

The Real Sufferer.

"Your husband seems to be the victim of the tobacco habit."

"No; I'm the victim. He thoroughly enjoys it."

Worse Still.

Wife (bitterly) - You deceived me when you married me.
Husband - I did more than that. I deceived myself.

Ahead of Him.

Mr. Sprockett - "You are improving in your bicycle riding, then?"

Miss Bloomer - "Oh, yes; I rode over five miles today and I kept ahead of your brother all the way."

Mr. Sprockett - "You don't say so!"

Miss Bloomer - "Yes; we were on a tandem."

What He Wanted.

Publisher (impatiently) - "Well, sir, what is it?"

Poet (timidly) - "Oh - er - are you Mr. Jobson?"

Publisher (irritably) - "Yes."

Poet (more timidly) - "Mr. George Jobson?"

Publisher (excitedly) - "Yes, sir, that's my name."

Poet (more timidly still) - "Of the firm of Messrs. Jobson & Doodle?"

Publisher (angrily) - "Yes. What do you want?"

Poet - "Oh, I want to see Mr. Doodle."

A Matter of Inference.

Cuttan Thrust - That young Dumleigh has got more money than sense.

Dulham Bluntly - I didn't know he was rich.

Cuttan Thrust - He isn't.

Dry.

"How do you like the new professor's lectures?"

"They seem extraordinarily dry considering how many founts of knowledge he has."

His Promise.

Husband - When we were married you were very thin, and weighed just a little over one hundred. Since then you have gained in flesh and weigh nearly two hundred. I'm positively ashamed of you.

Wife - You shouldn't be. You promised to love me through thick and thin.

Dyspepsia.

Mr. Newwed - There is no use talking, I won't eat any more of your cooking!

Mrs. Newwed (tearfully) - And you - you - said - you were willing to - die -die for me!

Mr. Newwed - But madam, there are worse things than death.

Icy Indifference.

"I'm afraid that after being friends for so many years those two girls have quarreled beyond reconciliation."

"They have beyond a doubt," replied Miss Cayenne. "I told one that I had just seen the other, and she didn't even ask me what she had on."

Mama's False Hair.

"Well, Lil; how do you like your new governess?"

Lil - "Well enough, ma; but she's so untidy. She doesn't even take her hair off when she goes to bed, like you."

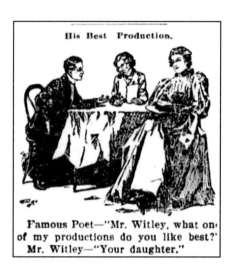

His Best Production.

Famous Poet—"Mr. Witley, what on of my productions do you like best?' Mr. Witley—"Your daughter."

How They Work.
"Do you find your fly-screens useful, Mrs. Podger?"
"Yes; the flies are so busy trying to get into the house that they don't bother us when we sit on the porch."

Heated Discussion.
"It was a pretty hot debate, wasn't it?"
"Well, several of the speakers were branded as liars."

A Brilliant Solution.
Chapleigh - What's the good of putting a steeple on a church?
Dudleigh - Where else would you put them, dear boy?
Chapleigh - That's a fact! Never thought of that!

The Responsibility.
Bass - Was that baby talk your wife was talking as I came in?
Fogg - That was mother talk; no baby I ever saw indulged in such gibberish.

A Harrowing Wit.
"I say, ma'am, won't you give me one of them famous pies of yours? I ain't had a square meal for a month. Do you think you could make a square meal out of one of my pies? Yes, ma'am, I just do."
"Well, you couldn't - my pies are all round!"

Canine Calisthenics.
Miss Primrose - Don't you ever give your dog any exercise?
Miss Hollyhock (fondling a fat pug dog) - Why, certainly. I feed him candy every few minutes, just to make him wag his tail.

A Flyer.
"Did your new machine fly, Hopely?"
"Yes; flew all to pieces as soon as I turned on the power."

A Resemblance.
A small boy, after critically surveying the new baby, remarked to his mother: "He's got no teeth and no hair. He's grandfather's little brother, ain't he, ma?"

Wisdom for Women.

"I think a woman should always allow someone else to choose her husband."

"What is your reason?"

"So she won't have to blame herself if he doesn't turn out well."

Must Wear Something.

Myra - That Miss Beare puts on a good deal of style when she goes to the opera.

Minnie - Well, good gracious! The woman's got to put on something!

Circumstances Rule.

Miss Belle - No, Mr. Poorman, I cannot marry you. Why, you are at least ten years my senior!

The next night: Miss Belle - Old, Mr. Gotrox? No. What is twenty years between you and me? I will marry you gladly.

"Are you ready for the hot weather, Mrs. Nobbs?"

"No; I haven't hid the thermometer yet."

It Seemed to Fit.

"Shakespeare must have had Miss Fussy's home-made root beer in mind."

"When?"

"When he talked about something being stale, flat and unprofitable."

The Widow's Bite.
"Dawson declares that if he marries at all he will wed a widow."
"Yes, that is like him; he is too lazy to do any of the courting himself."

All in His Head.
Professor - Give me the names of the bones that form the human skull.
Medical Student - I've got them all in my head, but I can't recall their names.

At the Raines Club.
"It strikes me," said the severe-looking stranger, "that this club was organized simply to sell beer to the members."
"Not at all," said the cheerful waiter, who was handing around the foaming schooners. "One of the rules forbids members to drink beer on the premises, and every time a man breaks that rule we fine him five cents."

He "Checked" It.
Wife, excitedly - If you go on like that I shall certainly lose my temper.
Husband - No danger, my dear, a thing of that size is not easily lost.

A Pleasing Definition.

"They tell me that that old fool of a Simpson is going to marry a girl of 18. He's 50 if he's a day."

"Yes. It's what he calls striking a sensible average."

Making Capital.

Mrs. Homer - Why don't you get something to do? Don't you know that doing nothing is the hardest kind of work?

Meandering Mike - And yet, lady, there is them what says we ain't an industrious class.

A Saving Son.

"John, this is a very bad report you bring me from school."

John - "I know, father; but you said if I brought home a first-class report you would give me $5, and I wanted to save you that expense."

Very Particular.

"Particular about her appearance! Well, I should say she was."

"What makes you think so?"

"Why, I happened to know that she spent over two hours dressing herself to sit for an x-ray photograph."

A Bit of Finesse.

"Dr. Blister has ordered Mrs. Flighty to the mountains for the summer."

"Did she need a rest?"

"No; he wanted a rest himself."

Judge - I think I have seen you before.

Prisoner - I have had the honor, your honor. I shaved, your honor, last week.

Judge - Twenty years.

How Extremes Met.

"Did her husband come up to her ideal?"

"No; her ideal came down to her husband."

He Was Bird.

Aide, charging furiously up - General, the enemy has captured our left wing. What shall we do?

The Command - Fly with the other.

An Advantage.

"I envy her her complexion," said Maud.

"But she freckles and tans so easily," replied Mamie.

"That's just it. She can go to the sea shore for a few days, and at the end of the season look exactly as if she had been away all summer."

A Needed Explanation.

Magistrate - Do you mean to say that such a physical wreck as he is gave you that black eye?

Complaining Wife - Sure, your honor, he wasn't a physical wreck until after he gave me the black eye.

A Case of Necessity.

First Chappie - My dear boy, you should never laugh at your own jokes.

Second Chappie - Oh, confound it, I've got to! I could never stand the everlasting silence that comes after them.

Evasion.

Miss Rivalle - Now Mr. Jones, I'm sure you think Miss Minks pretty?

The Astute Jones - Yes; she is pretty tall.

Changed Her Mind.

He - They say that even the most stupid of men know something.

She - I used to think so.

The Reason.

"I'm writing to Belle."

"Because you have something special to say?"

"No; because I have nothing special to do."

She - Mr. Detrop has dropped out of my life forever.

He - Elevator or coal hole?

The Cozy Flat Reception Room.

Mrs. Flatleigh, examining their new piano, regretfully - Oh, Reginald, the agent didn't give us any piano stool!

Mr. Flatleigh, philosophically - Never mind, dear, you can

sit on the sofa on the opposite side of the room and play nicely.

An Estimate.
Father - In asking for the hand of my daughter, young man, I trust that you fully realize the exact value of the prize you seek?
Prospective Son-in-Law – Well – er - I hadn't figured it quite so close as that, but I guessed it at about $500,000.

Eight-Year-Old - "Don't you know yet that the sun is ever so much bigger than the earth?"
Six-Year-Old - "Then why doesn't it keep the rain off?"

Fatherly Advice.
"Never be ashamed to apologize my son," said the Cornfed Philosopher to the hot-headed youth. "It is the gentlemanly thing to do, and besides, when a friendly footing is re-established, you have a chance to insult the other fellow again."

A Clash at Arms.
"Well, Bobby, have you had a pleasant day?"
"Yes ma'am; me and Jack took our three pups and went over to play with Bill Perkins' four cats."

Too Dreadful to Think Of.

Policeman—Come now, run along, you've been hanging round here all the morning!

Boy—See here, a man wot wears a belt o' your size can't cut no ice by being sassy. Where'd yer be if I wus to butt yer in the stummick wid all me might an' den run—eh?

A Matter of Necessity.

Mrs. Fussenfeather - I understand that Mr. Tallman kissed you on the stoop last night.

Miss Fussenfeather - Why yes, mama; he's so tall he had to.

Miss Wallflower - That gentleman over there has admired me all the evening. Who is he?

Her Friend - He is a collector of antiquities, dearest.

After a woman has been married a few months she goes around with a look on her face indicating that she smells a rat.

Not a Habit.

"I see that some scientist claims that death is largely a matter of habit, depending upon thought and all that," he said.

"Nonsense," she replied. "Did you ever know anyone who was in the habit of dying?"

Life in a "Flat."

The narrow quarters to which city people who live in "apartments" consign themselves are nicely indicated by a story told by a contemporary. In a certain city flat, the wallpaper had grown very dingy, but the landlord had persistently refused to replace it. At last the tenant said to his wife:

"It's no use, Julia, we shall have to put on some new paper at our own expense.

"And take all the trouble to scrape off the old?"

"Certainly no. We'll put it on right over the other."

"John! And make the rooms smaller still?"

Taking No Chances.

Mr. Curtis - "Yes. I must positively go back tomorrow morning."

Miss Emily - "Oh, I'm so sorry for that. I wish you could stay over for another day at least. You know we are going to give our performance of 'Camille' tomorrow night, with me in the title role."

Mr. Curtis (absently) - "That's the reason I've got to go."

"Joblots knows how to please lady customers."
"What does he do?"
"Calls all the married women 'Miss.'"

"Why," the young man asked, "Do you think that Miss Ashley will never be the wife of anyone but Harry Hinkley?"
"Because," the fair widow replied, "her parents are both strongly opposed to her having anything to do with him."

Why They Smile.
A hotel keeper near New York city is a Frenchman and his family knew little more about English than he does. His suburban hotel stands in the center of a yard filled with large trees. When the proprietor wanted to call attention to this advantage, he put on cards, "The best shady hotel around New York." The reputation of the place is beyond reproach and the proprietor does not know yet why so many persons smile when they read that line.

"My wife will be the first Klondike widow."
"Why, are you going?"
"No; but I am being talked to death by men who want to borrow money to get there."

When a girl who has pretty feet lies down in a hammock she always goes to lots of trouble to cover them up - and doesn't.

"A child in the house," said the thoughtful Chap, "is a joy forever."

"Yes," remarked the Nonsensical Guy somewhat sadly, "and I know people who are overjoyed."

A Matter of Colors.

"Sister Millie wants to know if you won't let us take your big awning? She's going to give a porch party tomorrow night and wants to have it."

"Wants my awning?"

"Yep. She would have borrowed the Joneses', but theirs is blue, you know, and Millie's hair is red."

He Gave Two.

A man had been up for an examination in the Scriptures, had failed utterly, and the relations between him and the examiner had become somewhat strained.

The latter asked him if there were any text in the whole bible he could quote. He pondered a moment and then repeated: "And Judas went out and hanged himself."

"Is there any other verse you know in the whole Bible?" the examiner asked.

"Yes. 'Go thou and do likewise.'" There was a solemn pause, and the proceedings terminated.

Dead to the World.

"You have just ruined my life," he said bitterly, just after she had broken the engagement. "My ambition is dead. I go to seek everlasting oblivion."

Then he became vice-president of the United States and was never heard of again.

"What has become of that man who gave memory lessons?"
"Oh-he hanged himself because his pupils forgot to pay his tuition bills."

They were looking over the prize fighter and enumerating his good points.
"How's his wind?" asked the visitor at last.
"Excellent," replied his manager. "He can outtalk a phonograph."

"Mr. Hawkins," said she, "I wish you'd decide a bet between me and Mr. Barrows. He says it is only 500 feet from here to the hotel, and I say it is 1,000 feet."
"Well," said Hawkins, "I should say you were both right. It's about 500 of Barrow's feet and 1,000 of yours."

"Oh, dear," sobbed Mrs. Hunnimune, "I knew it would come to this, but I didn't expect it so soon."
"Has your husband been mistreating you?" asked her visitor solemnly.
"Y-yes," she sobbed. "He says I want my own way all the time."
"And won't he let you have it?"
"That's the worst of it. He says that he doesn't care if I have my own w-way all the time, b-but that I won't make up my mind wh-what it is."

The Poor Man.
A little girl was looking out of a window the other day, says the Cleveland "Leader" when a man with a wooden leg limped past. "Oh, mama, mama!" cried the child, "come and see the man who walks with one foot and a curtain pole."

Moved Clear Out.
"My husband is never moved a bit by the pathetic scenes of a play. Is yours?"
"Oh, yes! They generally move him clear out of the house."

The Irony of Fate.
"It's hard," said the menagerie Lion.
"What's hard?" asked the kangaroo.
"To be starved when I'm alive, and stuffed when I am dead."

Handicapped.
"That man," remarked an admiring friend, "has the faculty of saying clearly in a few words what others would require pages to express."
"Too bad!" said Senator Sorghum, "He'll never get along in politics; not unless he learns to filibuster better than that."

Couldn't Be Mistaken.
"What makes you think you are his first love?"
"His lack of experience is so apparent."

Wouldn't Talk.

"Now, professor, I want you to tell me exactly what you think of my voice," said the young man with musical aspirations.

"No, sir," was the emphatic reply. I see through it, you were sent her by my enemies to get me arrested for profanity."

The Way She Saw Europe.

The friends of a girl who was just home from Europe were surprised to find when they questioned her about it the other day that there was a great deal she had left undone. "No, it was too much trouble to go to those out-of-the-way holes," she said, "and as for sight-seeing I never did care for it, anyway, so I soon made up my mind that I wasn't to wear myself out for all the old castles and art galleries that ever lived. But I had a good time; oh! Perfectly splendid! Just the very best I ever had in my whole life. Why, I couldn't help but have it. Didn't I spend all of my money?"

The Reason Is Plausible.

Morgan - I wonder why it is that priests never get married?
Flower - Don't you know that women have to confess their imperfections to the priest?
Morgan - Yes, of course; but -
Flower - Then what makes you ask such fool questions?

When a woman says of another woman, "She is very pretty," she expects her husband to speak up promptly and say: "She is not half as pretty as you are."

And Now?
Visitor - Well, I suppose you find comfort in the thought that you made your husband happy while he lived.
Young Widow - Oh, yes. I'm sure George was in heaven up to the time of his death.

That Clever Boy.
"Father," said the thoughtful little boy, "how many feet has a dog if we call his tail a foot?"
"Why, five, my son."
"No, father, that is not right."
"How so?"
"Why, he would only have four feet. You see, calling his tail a foot doesn't make it a foot."

It Wasn't Sudden.
"I suppose when you proposed to her she said 'This is so sudden.'"
"Not much. She said, 'Well, I think it is about time.'"

Anticipation.
Ruth - Did you enjoy your visit to New York?
Naomi - Splendidly, I was thinking all the time how nice it would be to get back to dear old Boston.

Mother (angrily)—Joe Jefferson! How many times muss I call yo', befo' I can make yo' hear?

Joe Jeff—Dunno—Yo' stan' thah an' holler, an' I'll sit here an' count.

He Had Studied Them.

"He says he has no head for figures."

"It is true."

"And yet he spent his time this summer on the bathing beach."

"Well, he didn't say he had no eyes for figures."

In the Same Boat.

"I want to know your intentions, sir," said the old man to the youth who had been calling on his daughter with great regularity for a long time.

"Same here," replied the young man promptly, "I'd like to know yours."

There is only one way in which a woman can get her revenge on a man and that is to marry him, but it is at a terrible cost to herself.

Even Worse.

She - "Don't you know anything worse than a man taking a kiss without asking for it?"

He - "I do."

She - "What, for instance?"

He - "Asking for it without taking it."

In Local Shipping Circles.

Diggs - "What's your friend Guzzle doing now?"

Biggs - "He's operating a line of schooners."

Diggs - "Between what points?"

Biggs - "The bar and his mouth."

Avoiding Distinction.

First Burglar - I'll have to get a bike soon.

Second Burglar - What for?

First Burglar - Well, if I don't I'll soon be known to the police as the only man in the perish what don't ride.

'Tis Strange Indeed.

"I saw a man who has no hands today play the piano."

"That's nothing. We have got a girl down in our flat who has no voice and who sings."

Another Point of View.

"There is altogether too much liberty allowed in this country. Look at our public streets, there is no safety there for man or beast."

"I thought the streets were full of safeties, but what is the matter now?"

"Our dog got out in the roadway, where he has a perfect right to be, and just because he wouldn't get out of the way quick enough to oblige a desperate wheelman he was run over and had his tail half amputated. It is an outrage and somebody will have to pay for it."

"What are you going to do?"

"I am going to sue the fellow who ran over him."

"Where is he?"

"He is still in the hospital."

He Lost the Wrong Leg.

Abraham Sprawls was a veteran of three great wars, and he used to live in Wiregrass, Georgia. He had lost one leg in a battle and walked around on a wooden stump. One day he got in the way of the fast mail and the engine ran over him. One of his sons - and he had a family of fifteen - had witnessed the accident, and running toward him, shouted: "Train's cut off dad's leg, an' he'll get damages!"

He lifted the old man to inspect his wounds, but suddenly let him fall saying in a tone of disgust:

"Durn it all! It's his wooden leg they've cut off!"

"Yes," groaned the old man, as they wheeled him home, "it's just my durned luck. Can't see ter save me how they missed the good leg."

Fine Potatoes.

The late Professor Jowett, during his connection with Balliot College, had occasion to visit some of the farms belonging to the college near the Scottish borders. One of the leading tenants was deputed to take the professor around. A long tramp they had, in the course of which Jowett uttered not a word, while the farmer was too stricken with awe to venture a remark. But when the walk was almost ended, the professor was roused to speech. Looking over a stone wall, over a goodly field of vivid green, he abruptly said: "Fine potatoes."

Quoth the farmer: "Yon's turnips."

Not a word more was spoken between them.

Stretching the Truth.

Stranger (in Arkansas) - So the poor fellow swore that he didn't steal the horse, and after you lynched him you found he had told the truth about it?

The Storekeeper - Yes; and the coroner was right smart puzzled what kind of verdict to bring in, but finally he called it 'a case of stretching the truth' and let it go at that.

Where Then?

Mrs. Benhem - In the next world people will be doing the same as in this.

Benhem - I don't believe it. How? I am a night clerk. How am I to get work in my life if I go where there is no night?

Mrs. Benhem - You won't go there.

Time Worketh Changes.

Wife - What makes you so anxious to go to Klondike? A week ago, you were very much against it.

Husband - But the baby wasn't teething then.

In Omaha.

First Thespian - When I was playing Hamlet in Omaha, and getting my fifty a night, I -

Second Thespian - Hold on there, Jack, make it five.

First Thespian - No, Tom, upon my honor, fifty a night regular. Eggs are cheap out there.

She Might.

"Could you learn to love me?" he asked.

"I don't know," she answered thoughtfully, "The cause of education is making great strides ahead these days and it is possible to learn almost any old thing."

A Humane Woman.

The Cabman - Gimme your bag lady and I will put it on top of the cab.

Mrs. Oatcake (as she gets in) - No; that poor horse has all that it can pull, I will carry it on my lap.

"Ah, if I could sail through life with you, dear one, by my side, like yonder yacht breasting the brine as she heels to the -"

"But that's just the trouble, Augustus. You aren't well enough heeled, papa says."

"There's money in stocks," said the man who is young and enthusiastic.

"Yes," replied his seasoned friend. "I'm sure there is. I have been putting half my salary there for the last four years, and that's all there yet."

"Did you ever find a man under the bed?"

"Once."

"Goodness me, where was that?"

"I was in the top berth of a sleeping car."

Dobbs – Maria, that beast of a dog of yours must go. She has just bitten a piece out of the calf of my leg.

Maria – Oh, this is too terrible!

Dobbs – It is a comfort to have some sympathy for once.

Maria – I was not thinking of you at all, but the veterinary surgeon yesterday ordered poor Floorie to be restricted to a milk diet.

Well Hardly.

"Compared with the care of a house you must find flat life very free and easy."

"Free? Well, I should say not. You forget about the janitor."

Many a man has been arrested for forgery simply because he has tried to make a name for himself.

Her Bad Arm.

Hewett - Does your wife miss you when you are away?

Sewett - She misses me when I am at home.

Hewett - What do you mean?

Sewett - She can't throw a cup straight.

His Answer.

Miss Oldmayde (coquettishly) - And you are sure you will love me when I am old?

Accepted Suitor (surprised) - Of course I will, I do now, don't I?

Her Interest in the Game.

"I'm sorry the baseball season is over," she said, thoughtfully.

"Were you interested in the game?"

"Not in the game itself. But I like to go with my husband and hear him cheer and cheer. It was the only time I knew that man to exhibit anything like a cheerful disposition."

"Well I am afraid poor Professor Andree is gone up."

"I think it more likely has come down."

"What is the precise status of a 'friendly power?' asked the seeker of knowledge.

"As a rule it's one you are too big to be whipped by." replied the cynic.

A Sure Sign.

"When a woman," said the corn-fed philosopher, "says that she really believes she is getting fat, and he husband retorts that it is because she eats too much and doesn't do enough work, it is safe to presume that the honeymoon has ceased to be."

"Nature has gone into the theatrical business."
"How so?"
"Look at the display of bare limbs."

A near-sighted man can manage to see over his neighbor's back fence.

So Sudden.

"Mr. Tillinghast left me $50,000," remarked the interesting widow to young Hilow

"My dear Mrs. Tillinghast," replied Hilow, "you should husband your resources."

"Oh, Frank, dear, this is too sudden. But are you really sure you love me?"

Out in Ohio the other day two football teams became involved in a row over the rules and resorted to a pitched battle in which clubs and stones were freely used. As this necessitated a postponement of the game, no one was seriously injured during the day.

Explained.

"What is studying human nature, uncle Alex?"

"Watching other people whom we don't think know how to behave as well as we do."

The farmer enhances the value of his possessions by soiling them.

Not Hampered.

"Would you be mean enough to give a bad piece of money to a blind man?"

"Of course; he can pass it off with a better conscience than I can."

A Mere Trifle.

Craig - Scribe lives on less than any man I know.

Biddle - I don't understand how he lives at all.

Sage - Why, he is living on the profits from the books he wrote on "How to Live Cheaply."

He had presented a lace collar to the lady of his heart and said in a jocular way: "Mind you don't crush it darling."

"No," she said demurely, "I will always take it off when you are here.

He took the hint.

Extra Hazardous.

"Is it for fire or life, sir, you want to take out a policy?" "Neither. I want to insure against accident. You see, I've married the strong woman from the Aquarium."—Ally Sloper's.

"I hope the book will be a success," said the author doubtfully, "but this is a severe blow to me."
"What is it?" asked his friend.
"The court has decided that the book is not immoral."

Corroborated.
"Here is more evidence that the pen is mightier than the sword."
"What is it?"
"Divorce papers can be written with a pen."

A Rival.
Don't ever give a dog to her.
Tis fatal, for 'tis true.
Ere many days that measly cur
Will have supplanted you.

Resigned to His Fate.

"Hello, Jerry: got your new flat all fitted up?"

"Not quite. Say, do you know where I can buy a folding tooth brush?"

Mrs. Yeast - Did your husband stand up on the car all the way home last night?

Mrs. Crimsonbeck - I don't see how he could. That was impossible even after he got home.

A Mismanaged Compliment.

Miss Passleigh - I consider it an insult.

Her Friend - You don't refer to that immense bunch of roses?

Miss Passleigh - I do. It is a birthday present and the card on it said, 'May each of these beautiful flowers represent a year of your life.'

Unlucky Thirteen

Perry Pattettic - You are not fool enough to believe in this fool thirteen superstition I hope?

Wayworn Watson - Why shouldn't I believe in it? Only last winter I got into cell 13 in one of them jails and instead of their keeping me good and warm for the winter they turned me out and gimme orders to leave.

A preacher in South Carolina asserted that "moonshining" is not a sin against God and the membership of his church tripled in one week.

His Wife's Comment.

He - The sight of an old schoolmate is - er well, it might be called both meat and drink.

She - Yes, that's what you men usually do under the circumstances.

He - Eh?

She - Meet and drink.

The Judge Robbed.

A Texas judge was robbed of a horse not long ago. The thief being apprehended was brought before him for trial. The judge eyed him with deep satisfaction for a minute or two and then delivered himself of the following: "Owing to personal prejudice, the court will not hear this case. It will be tried by the bailiff, who will find a verdict in accordance with facts. In the meantime," he added impressively, "the court will go outside and bend a rope and pick out a good tree."

A Kansas girl who lost her boa finds it impossible to lose her beau who sticks like wax.

Closing the Season.

"At any rate, my wheel is of the latest pattern."

"Yes. I have noticed that it usually gets in last."

Could Well Believe It.

Wallace - Hear about that young woman elocutionist who ran away from home because home was so unhappy?

Ferry - A young woman elocutionist? You can just bet her home was unhappy.

Not as Bad as Usual.
"Her Marriage must have been a terrible blow to her family."
"Blow? They didn't spend a cent; she ran away I tell you."

He Was Out.
The Customer - I think I will take some calves' brains today.
The Waiter - Sorry sir, but I haven't any brains today, sir.

A Feminine Attack.
When a woman wants to give an underhanded swipe at another woman she makes fun of her dressmaker.

"There are things in this world more valuable than money, my son."
"I know it, that is the reason I want the money to buy them with."

"How dreadful in Dr. Smith to marry his cook."
"I don't know, probably she had threatened to leave."

A Warning to Wives.

A Chicago girl tried to commit suicide because she did not like her new hat. This should be a warning to other women folks. Don't invite trouble by getting new hats.

Probable.

"I wonder what it is that creates such a prejudice against children in boarding houses."

"Boarding house children I guess."

Mothers-in-Law in Abyssinia.

Abyssinia's social code provides for a fair chance to young married couples by forbidding the bride's mother to visit her daughter till a year after the marriage.

She Appeals.

"John," said the wife of the citizen who had just settled his freak election bet like a little man, "the next time you want to bet on an election, just agree that, in case you lose, you won't make a fool of yourself for three months. It will be quite as difficult as anything else you could undertake, and it will spare the feelings of your relatives."

Boss Barber - Won't you wait, sir? It is your turn next.

Commercial Salesman - I can't spare time to wait until all of those fellows get their hair cut.

Boss Barber - But those men are all getting shaved; you see, sir, that this is a football town.

His Mission.

A clergyman famous for his begging ability was once catechizing a Sunday school. When comparing himself, the pastor of the church, to a shepherd and his congregation to the sheep, he asked the following question to the children. "What does the shepherd do for the sheep?"

To the amusement of those present a small boy in the front row piped out:

"Sheers them!"

Useful Books.

If a scholar has little money for books he should expend it mostly on works of reference, and so get a daily return for his output. So seems to have thought a young man of whom we recently heard, who, when asked by a canvasser to purchase an encyclopedia, said he had one.

"Which one is it?" inquired the canvasser.

The young man could not remember. Neither could he tell who published it; but it was a fine work, in many large volumes.

"Do you ever use them?" asked the agent.

"Certainly; almost every day."

"In what line?"

"Oh, I press my trousers with them. They are splendid for that.

It seems odd that a woman can be a cracker-jack cook for the heathen at church festivals, yet always needs a hired girl to cook for her husband.

His Specialty.

"Does your son worry you by contracting debts?"

"He doesn't contract debts - he expands them."

A Brooklyn woman has been given a judgement for $65,000 as a compensation for her husband's alienated affections. This sum may buy them back.

Was a Leading Question.

"Now," remarked the attorney's wife as she sat down on his chest and gave his ear another twist, after a disagreement, "now I want to know who holds the reins in this house."

"Madam," said her husband faintly, but with true courage still, "I refuse to answer. That is a leading question."

Prodding Memory.

One new system of monomoniacs, like all other systems, fails of absolute perfection. John Backwith, the warehouse man, received a letter the other day, addressed in a round business hand, and bearing the Oakland postmark. He glanced at it, rubbed his forehead reflectively for a moment, and then, without opening the envelope, tore it into bits.

"Why did you do that?" asked the partner. "That might have contained something of importance."

"No, it didn't. I wrote it myself."

"Are you in the habit of writing letters to yourself?"

"Yes, I have to. Now, if I hadn't written that yesterday and mailed it, I should have forgotten that bunch of braid, two dozen pearl buttons and five yards of haircloth that I've got to go up town and buy right now. Once, though, I wrote a letter to myself about something I wanted to remember, and forgot to mail it for two weeks."

An Interesting Question.
Thieves at Port Chester, New York, stole a flight of stairs. It would be interesting to know if it was their first steps in crime.

An Illustration.
"What is a good opening, Uncle Solomon?"
"A good opening is a widow getting a position of housekeeper for a widower."

Unlawful Attractions.
"What engaging manners Billinger has!"
"Yes; and he is a married man."

Nothing Serious.
"What is going on in your house this morning Tommy?"
"Oh, it's just Bertie. When he was playing in the pantry he knocked the molasses jar off from the shelf and the nurse is combing his hair."

His Real Object.
"I see that a New York preacher wants to abolish Santa Clause."

"Oh, no that isn't his object."

"What do you mean?"

"He just wants to get his name in the papers."

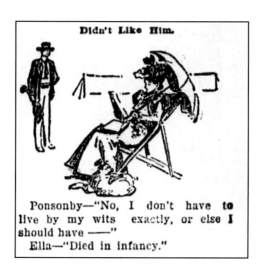

Ponsonby—"No, I don't have to live by my wits exactly, or else I should have ——"

Ella—"Died in infancy."

Poor, but Honest.

"My opponent" shouted the orator, "has seen fit to refer to the fact that my mother took in washing. She did and what is more to the point she always took it back."

After that there was nothing to do but cast a majority vote for the man whose parent showed such evidence of honesty.

A Kansas City Irishman declares that he never loses his temper; he always keeps it with him.

'Tis the Gun.

"Why is it that Chumpley always buys another new gun at the opening of the game season?"

"Because the one he had the year before never killed anything."

His Sorrow.

Guyer - "Where is Downtrod?"

Cheewit - "I left him alone with his sorrow."

Guyer - "Why, I thought his wife was dead."

Trouble About a Book.

A Connecticut man who received a bill for a book that he had no recollection of having ordered sent the following answer: "I never ordered the book. If I did, you did not send it. If I got it, I paid for it. If I didn't, I won't."

Where They Differ.

"No, sir," said the rabid free thinker, "the idea that there is a God has never for a moment entered my head."

"Same way with my dog, but he doesn't go around howling about it," replied the deacon.

A Discriminating Nurse.

Kind Lady - I am sure you would love my children.

Nurse - What wages do you pay?

Kind Lady - Fourteen dollars a month.

Nurse - I am afraid madam, I could only be affectionate with them at that price.

Simple but Effective.

"How did you succeed in simulating insanity so perfectly?" asked the friend of an escaped convict.

"I bought a catalogue of popular songs and repeated the titles one after another over and over."

Discussing the Year.

Tom - Statistics show a great increase of lunacy this year.

Dick - Well this has been an off year.

Prehistoric Barbecues.

"Major, did you read about them there discovering the bones of the mastodon down in the old state today?"

"I did colonel; thank you. What barbecues they must have had in those days, sir."

Cobwigger - I understand Terwill has broken a leg. Did you hear how it happened?

Meritt - He bought a horse that was advertised to be so gentle that a woman or child could handle it.

His Loquacious Wife.

Van Wither - How cheap things are getting to be. I see you can buy a talking machine for $10.

Van Miner - Yes, but I got one for nothing. It was a wedding present from my wife's parents.

Military Circles.
"So you are going away Mrs. Rusher?"
"Yes, we are going to move to Kentucky for a few weeks until my husband gets to be called 'colonel,' and then we shall go to Washington to live."

A Problem Plan.
"I believe you describe your new play as a problem play."
"Yes," replied the theatrical manager. "That's what the author said it was going to be, and for once he knew what he was talking about. Making the receipts cover the railway and hotel bills keeps me doing arithmetic 24 hours a day."

Can This Be True.
He - These shoemakers are pretty well up to the vanity of women. I have it on good authority they hit on the trick of putting smaller numbers in women's shoes.
She - Yes; and it also said that the hatters are numbering men's hats a size larger. There!

"I would like to know why I should feel jubilant over the outcome of this case?" exclaimed the enraged client.
"Didn't we obtain a verdict of $10,000?" asked the lawyer.
"Yes, but you get about all of it. What good does it do me?"
"My dear sir, the other fellow feels just as bad as if every cent of it went into your pocket!"

Not to be Cheated.

Time was when there was only one chaise in the town of Mechanic Falls, and that one belonged to an old man of somewhat eccentric ways. One day a young man wanted to hire the chase to take his best girl to ride. The owner agreed, but nothing was said about the price. Toward nightfall the young man brought the chase back.

"How much is the damage?" he asked.

"Where did you go?" returned the old man.

The young man named the place.

"How far do you call that?"

"Twelve miles."

"Nope, it is only ten," said the old man.

"I tell you it is twelve good long miles. I have been over it times enough to know."

"I traveled that road before you was out of dresses. I tell ye it hain't but ten miles."

Both of them were losing their tempers rapidly.

Never mind how far it is, tell me how much I owe you and I will pay you and get out."

Catching his breath, the old man thundered: "Young feller, ye don't owe me a cent, but by mighty, I will be durned if ye are going to cheat me on the distance.

"You are short a cent," said the conductor as he leaned forward and breathed heavily.

"You are not," said Briggs as he caught an agonizing waft of garlic.

It was an afternoon tea; the crush was simply horrid. It seemed that nothing would save the few men present when one quick-witted woman exclaimed: "Ladies remember there are gentlemen in the crowd!" It was all that preserved the poor things from a horrible fate.

There is no pleasure in having nothing to do; the fun is in having lots to do - and not doing it.

She - I don't see what draws you men into politics. As for me, I can't make anything out of it.
He - It is the hope of making something out of it that makes many men go in.

"Once a friend of mine and I decided that it would be helpful for each of us to tell the other his faults."
"How did it come out?"
"We have not spoken for nine years."

"It is too bad they didn't have judges in Adam's time."
"Why?"
"Think of the trouble he might have saved by getting an injunction to restrain the angel from driving him out of the garden of Eden."

Bad Every Way.
Jarley - Thirteen is an unlucky number in all cases.
Butler - Oh, I don't know. I would rather have thirteen dollars than twelve.

Jarley - I wouldn't, for if I had twelve dollars I would only spend twelve, but if I had thirteen I'd spend thirteen.

Terrible.

New Boarder—"This rain is good for the farmer. Brings things up out of the ground, you know."

Farmer—"Gosh, don't talk that way. I've just buried my third wife."

A Relief Measure.

"What made that girl next door quit banging the piano so suddenly?"

"The neighbors took up a collection and bought her a box of paints."

Great Time for Extras.

Two newsboys in the gallery witness a performance of Hamlet. In the last scenes, after Hamlet has killed Laertes and the King, and the Queen has died of poison and Hamlet of a poisoned wound, one of the newsboys exclaimed, "Jim, what a time that must have been for extra specials!"

He Ate the Evidence.

A man was arrested in San Francisco the other day for catching fish below the unlawful weight.

"Where are the fish?" asked the attorney for the defendant.

"Why, they wouldn't keep," answered the officer.

"What did you do with them?"

"Oh, I disposed of them."

"What did you do with them?"

"Oh, I knew they would not keep so I-I disposed of them."

"But what did you do with them? Is the question."

"My wife cooked them."

"And you ate them?"

"Yes."

"Your honor I ask that this case be dismissed."

"Charge dismissed and defendant discharged," ruled the justice of the peace, "on the ground that the arresting officer at the evidence."

Enlightened.

Little Johnny - Papa, what's a pessimist?

Papa - A fellow who thinks other folks always tell the truth when they talk about the salaries they get.

Not in Danger of Oblivion.

"He devoted his immense fortune to the perpetuation of his memory."

"How?"

"He left it in such shape that every dollar of it will be litigated over."

They Acquitted.

"Gentlemen of the jury," said the lawyer impressively, "our defense is insanity. I will show that my client once served on a jury and listened to expert testimony for four months."

Jean - Why is it that you never speak of Mr. Outre? He is uncouth but I feel sure he is a diamond in the rough.

Katherine - So do I; that is the reason I am cutting him.

"A dyke is a sort of a dam, isn't it?"

"Yes; why?"

"Then I think that in view of the amount of profanity the Klondike has provoked its name should be changed to Klondam."

If Andree will promise not to lecture when he comes out of the wilderness of the Arctic, there can be no objections to sending out an expedition to bring him back; but he must promise.

He Considered the Workers.

Mr. Holiday - So you think you would like to take position of superintendent of the works? Don't you think it better for you to seek a more humble place at first?

Rollow - Why, sir, you have told me that there is always plenty of room at the top. Surely you would not have me crowd the worthy men who are lower down.

The Early Worm Again.

A father was lecturing his son on the evil of staying out late at night and rising late in the morning.

"You will never succeed, unless you mend your ways. Remember the early bird catches the worm," he said.

"And what about the worm, father? Wasn't he rather foolish to get up so early?" replied the young man sneeringly.

"My son, that worm had not been to bed at all; he was only just getting home."

The young man coughed.

Merely Her Way.

Geraldine - I never allow a man to kiss me unless we are engaged, but -

Gerald - But what?

Geraldine - Of course we can break the engagement after the kiss.

One Good Habit.

"Mrs Clingstone is always talking about the bringing up of other people's children. Are her own so wonderful??

"Well, I know her boy never goes out nights."

"Her boy? I never saw him."

"No, he is in the penitentiary."

If canes were to go out of fashion some young men would have no visible means of support.

The 'Old Man' Objected.

Jimmy - Say, Billy, why don't you let yer hair grow long and look like a football player.

Billy - I did started to, but the old man said if I went around looking like a mop, he'd wipe the floor with me.

Grateful.

"Doctor, I owe you my life," said the substantial citizen as he rushed up to the young physician.

"Eh?"

"I was taken suddenly ill yesterday and my wife sent for you and you were not in."

Mr. Asbery Pepper.

"My cousin's marriage was quite romantic," said the blond boarder. "He was wheeling along a country road last summer and went into a farmyard and the farmer's daughter, who was making bread, made such a pretty picture that he fell in love then and there."

"Many a woman," said Asbery Peppers, "has got married because she was needing dough."

All Over.

"My wife and I have our little quarrels once in a while, but they are all over in a few minutes," said the man who lives with others in the pasteboard flats.

"I presume you mean all over the house?" said the other man who had some experience in flat life.

Remedies for a Cold.

Wife - You'd better stay at home today, dear. You have such a cold.

Husband (Thinking well of the idea) - I don't know I guess-

Wife - You could clear the snow off the back porch, make a path to the hen house, and go to the store and get -

Husband - I guess I will go to the city.

Not A Free Citizen.

"Jones has moved back to the country."

"Why?"

"He said he wouldn't live in a town where the neighbors objected to his keeping his cow in the front yard."

A Safeguard.

Wallace - I didn't know you rode a bicycle.

Ferry - I don't.

Wallace - Then what are you wearing knickerbockers and a sweater for?

Ferry - To keep the bicycle riders from running over me. They think I am one of 'em.

A Literary Man.

Uncle George - So you think Mr. Caxton is a literary man?

Carrie - I am sure of it. When he wants to find anything in a book he wastes half an hour hunting for it before he thinks to look in the index.

Bound to be Modest.

"If a girl wears a bicycle skirt that comes to within two inches of the top of her shoes there can be no question as to her modesty, can there?" she asked.

"Certainly not," was the unsuspecting reply.

"Because I am very anxious to keep within the bounds of modesty and propriety."

The question being thus settled, she straightaway purchased a pair of bicycle button boots that reached to her knee."

A Bond of Sympathy.

There is, after all, nothing that unites two hearts more firmly than a mutual hatred for some third party.

Encouraging His Whim.

Irate Father - "I'm getting tired of this nonsense. You've been engaged to that young man for six months. Does he ever intend to marry you?"

Daughter - "You must have patience, papa. Remember he's an actor."

Irate Father - "What's that got to do with it?"

Daughter - "He's fond of long engagements."

She - Mr. Brown does not pay his wife much attention.

He - No; the only time I ever knew of his going out anywhere with her was once when the gas exploded.

Foolish Doubts.

"And now," said the client, as he was about to leave, "you really think I have a chance to win?"

"Haven't you confessed that you are penniless and haven't I agreed to take the case?" the lawyer asked. "What do you want - an affidavit?"

Horse-and-Horse.

Husband (after a cold night) - "Maria, I think the water pipes are all frozen up."

Maria - "Well, why don't you get a plumber before they bust?"

Husband - "Because I don't want the plumber to bust me!"

A Varied, Wild West.

"Yes, sir," thundered the man with the long, grizzled whiskers, "I am from the fairest land the sun ever kissed. I am from the west, gentlemen."

"Ah, yes; is that so?" inquired a bystander. "Are you from the malaria district, the grasshopper quarter, the tuberculosis section, the drought region, or the cyclone belt?"

If women were as fond of appearing in print as in silk there would be more lady writers.

Dame nature never fails to give every creature some weapon of offense and defense. She gave babies lungs and women tears.

121

No Opportunity to See.

Mother—Why don't you bring them pig's feet? Hasn't the butcher got 'em?

Son—How could I tell when he kept his shoes on all the time.

If Women Voted.

Mrs. Bildad (throwing down the paper) - "I declare! There is another horrid municipal scandal. Every man nowadays seems to have something to do with a ring."

Bildad - "And if women were given half a chance don't you think they would have their finger in it, too?"

How It Affected Her.

Dr. Blewmass - "I am surprised, Mrs. Brownjones, to hear you say you are a martyr to biliousness. You are the picture of health, and don't look as if you were subject to it."

Mrs. Brownjones - "Oh, I am not, but my husband is - that is the way I suffer from it."

One Better.
George - "When I marry, I want to get a girl as good as gold."
Charlie - "I think you'd aim to do even better than that."
George - "How?"
Charlie - "Get a girl who has the gold."

Matrimonial Bliss.
Kitty - "Ned and his wife get along nicely together. Her mother told me no words ever pass between them."
Jack - "Of course not. Ever since their quarrel they don't speak to each other."

And If He Lost His Mind.
Brown - "That is Billion over there; they say he is worth a million - it's in his mine."
Jones - "Yes, that's where my million is - in my mind."

Providential Perhaps.
Mr. Chump - "Love is blind."
Miss Sparkle - "That's fortunate for some men."

Not in Sight.
Percy Algernon - Aw, say, Miss Slydig, would you mind a man sitting down beside you on the divan?
Miss Slydig - Certainly not! But where is the man?

It All Depended.
An exchange says that a girl baby was brought to a clergyman in Syracuse, N.Y., to be baptized. The minister

asked for the name of the child, and the father responded, "Dinah M."

"But what does the 'M' sand for?" asked the clergyman.

"Well, I don't know yet," the father replied. "It all depends upon how she turns out. If she is nice and sweet and handy about the house, like her mother, I shall call her Dina May; but if she has a fiery temper, like mine, I shall call her Dinah Might."

He who devotes sixteen hours a day at hard study may become as wise at sixty as he thought himself at twenty.

A young man who fancies he dislikes his mother-in-law experiences a sudden revulsion of feeling when his first-born begins to lisp "Grandma."

When the unpaid grocer comes in at the door, romance flies out of the window.

Too Long.

A countryman walked into a newspaper office to advertise the death of a relative. "What is your charge?" he asked the clerk.

"We charge $2 per inch."

"Oh!" said the countryman, "I can't afford that. My friend was 6 feet 3 inches."

Contempt of Court.

A stranger once walked into a criminal court and spent some time watching the proceedings. By and by a man was brought up for contempt of court and fined, whereupon the stranger rose and asked: "How much was the fine?"

"Five dollars," replied the clerk.

"Well," said the stranger, laying down the money, "If that's all, I'd like to join in. I've had a few hours' experience in this court, and no one can feel a greater contempt for it than I do, and I am willing to pay for it."

It is difficult to tell which gives some couples the most happiness, the minister who marries them or the judge who divorces them.

An Indian reservation is a piece of land ceded to the red man with the reservation that if it is ever found to contain mineral wealth, or can be of any use whatever to the white man, the Indian must move on.

Some poet has said that angels are all blondes, but that doesn't prove that all the blondes are angels.

No Such Servant Girl.

Mr. Uptown (reading) - A prominent artist recently painted some cobwebs on his ceiling so realistic that the servant girl was overcome with an attack of nervous prostration in trying to sweep them down.

Mrs. Uptown - I don't believe there is a word of truth in that article.

Mr. Uptown - Why no, dear? There are any number of

artists capable of executing work like that.

Mrs. Uptown - That may be true, but there never was such a servant girl.

Waggles - I talked to him like a father.

Wiggles - It won't do any good if he listened to you like a son.

"Artemus," she cried hysterically, "I feel that something has come between us."

"Alicia," he replied, "it is my toothbrush it is forever slipping down my vest lining."

The Right Side.

"When I was in the country last summer I discovered a cow that is always milked on one side," remarked Hunker.

"And I know which side that is," replied Higgins, who had never been in the country in his life.

"Which?"

"The outside."

An Opinion.

Edith - Jack says his father threatens to disinherit him.

Marie - That is a mere bluff to make you think his father has money.

Too Good a Boy.

"Now, Edward, the best portions of the fowl are for the guests so what will you say when I ask you what you will have?"

Tramp - Is there anything around here that a poor man could do to earn a meal of vittles?
Lady - Yes, step back this -
Tramp - All right then, I haven't time to stop.

"Why did you ever come to this frozen country?" Asked one traveler of another in the Chilkoot pass.
"My creditors made it too hot for me in New York," replied the other through his chattering teeth.

"Those new neighbors seem to be great borrowers."
"Borrowers?"
"One night when they gave a dinner they borrowed our family album."

Femininity may be defined as the art with which a woman graciously permits a hapless man to apologize to her for some offence of hers against him.

A German writer says: "Almost all poets, artists or scholars have led a more or less unhappy domestic life." Now half the men in this world will imagine themselves great poets, artists, or scholars.

Hard to Tell.

"What an eccentric person old Fogg is," remarked one young man.

"Yes, but he is a great student."

"I know it. I have never been able to make up my mind whether he was twenty years ahead of time or twenty years behind."

Among the varied phenomena of every-day life, none exceeds in painful intensity the endeavors of a girl to keep step through the intricacies of a joke that has convulsed her fiancé.

Incompatible.

"Squallinger, what has become of your carriage and span of bays?"

"Had to sell them, Flickinger. I am keeping a baby carriage and a span of twins."

When a woman has fairly sat on a man, forever afterward the entire masculine race takes on the appearance of groveling upholstery.

The San Francisco woman who claims to have committed bigamy while under hypnotic influence was no different from many other women who get married without knowing what they are doing.

Taken for Granted.

"Tell me Rafferty, is Clancy still a walking delegate?" asked Mr. Dolan.

"No," was the reply.

"Are you sure?"

"Not that I have personal knowledge, but I take it for granted he's riding a hack by this time."

What a Spectacle.

Professor (of astronomy) - How many of the planets can be seen with the naked eye?

Dear Little Girl - I don't know, sir. We have no naked eyes in Boston.

The honcymoon usually ends where the burned steak begins.

A home without children is no doubt very peaceful and quiet, but so is a graveyard.

One-half the misery in the world is caused by men who drink and women who can't cook.

An Ohio girl tied her lover to a tree and went for a parson and had the marriage ceremony performed before the man was released. The girl evidently knew how to tie a beau knot.

His Youthful Logic.

Mrs. Figg - Tommy, I am horrified to think that you would cut the cat's tail off! Is that living up to the Golden Rule? Tommy - Course it is. If I had a tail I should want someone to cut it off.

A Rule.

"You have something of a reputation as a literary critic," said the deep man's confidential friend.

"Yes," was the reply, "that is easily attained. Whenever I find a book so interesting in plot that I can't lay it down -"

"You commend it?"

"No, I say it is rather clever, but it is not real literature."

He Told his Name.

He was dressed like a farmer, and he looked inquiringly at the clerk behind the counter of our chief post office, and pointed pantomimically to a bundle of letters the latter was sorting.

"What name?" asked the clerk.

"Louder," replied the agriculturist.

Supposing the man to be deaf, the clerk repeated his query in a tone calculated to wake the dead. But the man only smiled an unmeaning smile and said: "Louder."

The clerk took a long breath, and the yell that followed startled even the phlegmatic husbandman.

"No offense, sir, I hope? Yes, that's my name - Louder, sir."

"Oh, ah!" said the clerk; "I never thought of that. Yes, here is a letter."

DANGER AHEAD.

The Pug—Say, I'm in a fix.
The Poodle—What is that?
The Pug—If I turn up my nose at the bulldog, there'll be trouble. Yet how can I help it?—New York Evening World.

Proved His Calling.

"Well, old man, did your son pass the civil service examination?"

"No, sir - they turned him down."

"What was the trouble?"

"Short on arithmetic, sir."

"Anything else?"

"And geography."

"Yes."

"And spelling."

"Nothing more?"

"Nothing more, sir, except grammar and history, and a few other things."

"Well, sir, he has just about decided to teach school."

Not to be Buncoed.

"Madam," said the urbane canvasser, "I have here a handy little article that no well-regulated household should be without. It is at one time a paper-cutter, and envelope opener, a button hook, crochet needle, a corkscrew, a nut pick, a bodkin and many other things too numerous to mention. It is small neat and compact, and the price is but twenty-five cents."

The woman of the house looked him over contemptuously. "Huh!" she said. "Do I look like a fool enough to pay a quarter for a hairpin when I can get a whole pack of them for five cents?" And the door slammed in his face.

Bringing It Up to Date.

The Park commission was ordering a statue.

"I suppose you want this warrior mounted?"

"Yes, yes, of course," replied the spokesman. "He ought to be mounted unquestionably, but just now you had better confine your work to the figure of the man. We'll tell you later whether to put it on a horse or a bicycle."

In Willie's Midst.

Mother - Oh, doctor, what is the matter with him?"

Physician (with his hand on Willie's stomach) - Nothing serious. I think, madam, merely the annual Christmas gathering.

The Lesser Evil.

Wife - I tell you that marriage makes man more docile, more humane. Statistics show that sixty-five percent of our criminals are celibates.

Husband - My dear, your argument is against you. Your statistics simply show that celibates prefer prison to marriage.

What the Fence Was For.

Smart Tourist - I say there, friend, what are you building a wire fence around that field for? There isn't anything in there that any animal could possibly eat.

Farmer - Huh! Reckon I know what I'm about, sonny. I'm putting up this fence for fear some of my cows might stray in there and starve to death.

~~~~~~

Sanctum Mysteries.

Humorist's Wife - What in the world are you sending all these jokes to the Daily Blowhard for? They are as old as the hills.

Humorist - Yes, my dear; but the editor who selects the humorous matter for that paper is a young fellow just out of college, and they'll be all new to him.

ABOUT.

Erin O'Reilly is an antique cookbook and newspaper hobbyist. This present collection is a compilation of jokes collected from American newspapers in the late 1800s. In her other life, she is a university administrator, mother, Army veteran, and amateur wine maker.

Manufactured by Amazon.ca
Acheson, AB

13483634R00081